W9-CRS-719

Telecourse Study Guide

FOCUS ON SOCIETY
SECOND EDITION

Paul Magee

X   9 6 0

Worth Publishers, Inc.

Focus on Society, Second Edition, Study Guide

Copyright © 1987, 1981 by Dallas County Community College District

All rights reserved

Printed in the United States of America

ISBN: 0-87901-375-3

First printing, June 1987

Cover: *La Place, Clichy* (detail), Louis Anquetin

Wadsworth Atheneum, Hartford, Connecticut

The Ella Gallup Sumner and Mary Catlin Sumner Collection

Unit 1, page 1: Paul Conklin, Monkmeyer Press Photos

Unit 2, page 41: Leif Skoogfors/Woodfin Camp & Associates

Unit 3, page 79: Tom Martin/The Stock Market

Unit 4, page 123: Van Bucher/Photo Researchers

Worth Publishers, Inc.

33 Irving Place

New York, New York 10003

Acknowledgments

The author extends thanks to the staff of the Center for Telecommunications, Dallas County Community College District (DCCCD), for valuable assistance in this project, especially to Pamela K. Quinn, Director; to Theodore Pohrte, Instructional Design Specialist; to Sandra Adams, Copy Editor.

My thanks go also to Dr. Margot Olson of North Lake College, DCCCD, for her expert advice in testing; to LaVada Pepper at Richland College, DCCCD; and to Joyce McDowell and the Tarrant County Junior College District for their friendly and generous assistance on content.

The *Focus on Society* telecourse is produced by the Center for Telecommunications of the Dallas County Community College District.

Contents

To The Student

In preparing this Study Guide, and in writing the lessons for the television element of the course, I have tried to keep in mind many of the thoughts, topics, and illustrations which have made this course interesting and even fun for myself and my students for more than a decade. Sociology is fascinating because it is a study of human behavior in groups of all kinds and of the many values, rules, and patterns which emerge from and guide that behavior. It is about our individual everyday lives—what we do, how we do it, and even why we do it and what it means to us.

The opening segment of each Study Guide lesson, titled "Sociological Perspective," has been kept deliberately informal, even casual. I hope by this approach to stir your interest and keep your attention, as well as to illustrate the many ways in which sociology concerns your life. This opening segment gives a brief glimpse of what is in the lesson. It is not an outline or summary of either the text or the TV program. It may occasionally be provocative, even controversial. I hope that it and the other course elements will encourage critical thinking and expand the intellectual and emotional dimensions of your life.

Unlike many academic works, but like many good books, there is a "kicker" at the end of this one. Lesson 30 is the best part. By then you will have finished your sociological tour of people, places, concepts, and problems. At the end you will be challenged to use what you have learned in the course to look ahead toward a New Society, to struggle intellectually and emotionally with the choices you have to make as a participant in a complex social system. You will share in the thinking of some brilliant and courageous people, past and present, who thought and continue to think deeply about the world they were and are part of, and who gave and continue to give of their knowledge and understanding.

You need not, in fact should not, believe everything you read or hear in this course. But you can learn from it. No student or instructor is value-free. But a good sociology course should clarify values, expand options, and break the sides out of the ruts in which we often live.

Many people have given generously of their time to make possible this unique opportunity to study sociology; many from colleges and universities across the United States; others from various walks of life—ordinary people who talked about their lives and who became part of the content of this course. Most of them gave far more than they received. The letters, phone calls, and cameras intruded into their private worlds. But those brief and personal glimpses of real people are what makes this course exceptional. When you have viewed their reality through the lenses of sociology, you, they, and I will be rewarded.

Paul Magee

STUDY GUIDE

Sociological Perspective

This is a brief and informal introduction to each lesson. It will guide you into some of the concepts to be used and will suggest some ways in which the sociology of the particular lesson relates to your life.

Learning Objectives

These state the expanded intellectual abilities you should have upon finishing the lesson, as well as some attitudinal changes which may or may not occur. Some of these relate to the reading and others to the television program.

Key Terms

These are among the most important terms used in the lesson. The definitions given in the Study Guide are at times more informal than may be found elsewhere. Most of these terms and many more are defined in the glossary of the text.

Reading Assignment

In all but four of the lessons, the reading assignment is in the text. In lessons 3, 20, 26, and 30, the reading assignment is in the Study Guide.

Reading Focus Questions

These questions relate to the text as well as to the Additional Readings, and to the learning objectives stated in the Study Guide.

TV Focus Questions

These questions relate to the television program and to the learning objectives stated in the Study Guide.

Optional Activities

These activities serve two purposes: (1) they assist in making practical connections between sociology and your life experiences, and (2) with specific agreement with your instructor, they may be done to earn extra credit.

Posttest

This provides you with an opportunity to check your comprehension of the material in the lesson. The questions relate to the learning objectives and thus are based upon both the readings and the television programs. The posttest also should be very useful in reviewing for examinations.

TEXT

There is one book required for this course: *Sociology*, Third Edition, by Ian Robertson (Worth Publishers, Inc., 1987). The reading assignments for each lesson are given by page numbers and are not necessarily sequential.

TELEVISION PROGRAMS

These programs consist of fresh, original interviews with experts in sociology, anthropology, political science, and related fields. There is much new film which illustrates the topics or concepts being discussed. There are appropriate on-camera sequences of the narrator that make transitions or summarize discussions. The television element of the course does not cover all of the material for each lesson. Typically, it introduces a basic concept or topic and then moves to examine a specific aspect of that area of sociology. It is vital that you read the text carefully for material not covered in the television program.

For maximum learning and efficiency of time use, there is a particular sequence which should be followed in studying each lesson. It is outlined in this check list.

1 ☐ Read the sociological perspective.

2 ☐ Read the learning objectives.

3 ☐ Study the key terms.

4 ☐ Read the text focus questions.

5 ☐ Read the text (or Additional Reading).

6 ☐ Study the important terms at the end of the text chapter.

7 ☐ Write answers to the text focus questions.

8 ☐ Read the TV focus questions.

9 ☐ Review the learning objectives.

10 ☐ Watch the TV program—make mental notes on important concepts, terms, or data (or some brief written notes).

11 ☐ Write answers to the TV focus questions.

12 ☐ Take the posttest.

13 ☐ Review the optional activities.

Telecourse Study Guide

FOCUS ON SOCIETY
SECOND EDITION

Sociology and Culture

The Promise of Sociology

SOCIOLOGICAL PERSPECTIVE

Imagine yourself sitting at your home computer with phone on the modem, reading on the screen information from a data bank. What an efficient and exciting way to write a term paper! Martin Luther should have had access to such powerful communication technology! While you are on line, you decide to ask for the day's headlines and note with interest that the "Baby M" surrogate mother case finally has been decided by the court. It causes you to wonder a bit about what human relationship will be affected next by the new technology.

A second item catches your eye. The state penal system is experimenting with a new method of managing convicts. It is called "electronic house arrest." Individuals convicted of nonviolent crimes and sentenced to jail terms are able to serve them not in jail but on a routine schedule which allows them to work, take their kids to the park, attend church. They are required to be in their residences at certain hours. The restrictions on their movements are enforced by a small electronic transmitter taped to an ankle and never removed for the duration of the sentence. Whatever happened to hard time!

Now the homework is finished and you switch on a large-screen TV with an incredible array of choices available on cable or through your satellite dish. Watching two games simultaneously or a game and your favorite action soap no longer requires channel hopping because you have the two-screen set and think of it as daily fare.

Now imagine individuals who cool milk in a glass jar in a stream in the summer, eat the evening meal by an oil lamp, and are in bed by eight o'clock because the day starts very early and there is little time for frivolous activities. The next day will be another long day of plowing or wood cutting for the men and of food canning or clothes washing for the women. Days are long and there is not much excitement in work.

These scenes could be rewritten to describe various times and circumstances in which people live or have lived: rich and poor, rural and urban, black and white, single and married. Whatever scene we examine, we would find people living in groups, dividing the labor, and creating rules to guide their lives. We would also find them responding to the conditions which surround their groups, whether the conditions are social, economic, political or ecological.

Whether we examine a society in which many individuals are bored, self-indulgent, alienated from work, family, community, and self, yet dependent

3

upon others for everything from a drink of water to education; or whether we examine a society where concerns are more closely related to survival, we find that prevailing conditions affect how individuals feel about themselves, the values they hold, and the behavior patterns which prevail in their daily lives.

Whatever scene we recall or merely imagine, basic human needs are essentially the same. The ways in which people go about meeting those needs, the obstacles which they encounter in doing so, and the nature of their encounters with other individuals make up part of the complicated picture which sociology tries to focus. Understanding the nature of social conditions, the ways in which relationships are structured, and the rules and value judgments under which life is conducted should help any individual cope with life more effectively.

This lesson is an introduction to the discipline of sociology, its major schools of thought, the kinds of activities in which sociologists engage as scientists, and the promise of understanding that is offered to the serious student of sociology. Here are some ideas which will explain what is happening in society and in yourself and will give you a better grasp of your life chances—and perhaps a better understanding of what makes you what you are.

LEARNING OBJECTIVES

Knowledge Objectives

1 Define sociology.

2 Identify early social theorists and their ideas.

3 Identify major theoretical orientations in sociology.

4 Describe various types of activities in which sociologists engage as scientists.

5 Describe various methods used by sociologists in studying society.

6 Describe "sociological imagination" as a point of departure for the study of society.

7 Describe changes in American culture from 1850 to 1985.

8 Identify three "payoffs" for the individual who studies sociology.

Attitudinal Objectives

1 Become more aware of and appreciate more fully the complexity of the life situation of all individuals.

2 Recognize more fully the extent to which individuals live in groups and are responsive to their environments.

KEY TERMS

Sociology   The scientific study of human behavior in groups and of the structure and function of society.

Theoretical orientation   A broad set of assumptions which form a perspective from which to examine society and social behavior.

Sociological imagination   A perspective of social realities which calls for the location of the individual's biography on the historical time line and raising certain questions which explain what is happening in society and in the individual.

Methodology   A system of principles and procedures which guide scientific investigation.

READING ASSIGNMENT

Robertson: *Sociology*, pp. 1–51

READING FOCUS QUESTIONS

1   What is sociology?

2   What is the "sociological imagination?"

3   Who are the early theorists in sociology?

4   What are the major theoretical perspectives in sociology?

5   What are the basic research methods used in sociology?

TV FOCUS QUESTIONS

1   What is the promise of sociology?

2   What is the "sociological imagination?"

3   What is the significance of the major "signs of our times" in understanding society today?

4   What years were the cultural watershed in America in this century?

5   What is the formal definition of sociology?

6   What do sociologists do?

7   What are the payoffs for the individual studying sociology?

8   What three questions may be asked by the sociological imagination which generate understanding of society?

OPTIONAL ACTIVITIES

1 Identify three major technological innovations in your lifetime and
   examine their impact upon your way of life and your behavior patterns.

2 Identify two major social issues in the United States. Make some brief
   notes on your thinking about the causes and solutions to these issues. File
   these in the back of your text and examine them near the end of the
   course to see if your perceptions have changed.

POSTTEST

Multiple Choice

1 The basic aim of sociology is the
   a. manipulation of human behavior.
   b. elaboration of common sense.
   c. application of the scientific method to a study of human behavior in
      groups.
   d. gathering of statistics about society.

2 The "father of sociology" was
   a. Emile Durkheim.
   b. Karl Marx.
   c. Auguste Comte.
   d. Max Weber.

3 Structural functionalists
   a. view all parts of society in terms of how they function to maintain
      social order and balance.
   b. focus on the processes of social change.
   c. concentrate upon individuals and their interpersonal relationships.
   d. examine social conflict.

4 The study of sociology is
   a. focused primarily upon unusual human behavior.
   b. very wide in scope and involves many topics and types of work.
   c. concerned largely with predicting human behavior.
   d. useful primarily in classroom teaching.

5 Durkheim's study of suicide indicated that
   a. group rates vary consistently.
   b. it is entirely individualistic.
   c. social forces are not influential.
   d. mostly insane people do it.

6 The sociological imagination asks about
   a. psychology and sociology.
   b. culture and language.
   c. biography and history.
   d. technology and industry.

7 The watershed years of 1930 to 1950 were
   a. stimulated by the "big war."
   b. a movement from rural to urban America.
   c. a time of change in work, credit, and education.
   d. all of these.

8 A major payoff for the student of sociology is
   a. higher job skills.
   b. a more attractive personality.
   c. a better understanding of self and society.
   d. an increased ability to manipulate others' behavior.

9 A major tool offered by the sociological imagination is
   a. an intellectual grasp of the complex issues in society.
   b. scientific research ability.
   c. an ability to resist depression.
   d. the power to predict others' behavior.

POSTTEST ANSWERS

1 c (obj. 1, TV, Text, p. 5)
2 c (obj. 2, Text, p. 13)
3 a (obj. 3, Text, p. 17)
4 b (obj. 4, TV, Text, p. 3)
5 a (obj. 5, Text, p. 15)
6 c (obj. 6, TV, Text, p. 6)
7 d (obj. 7, TV)
8 c (obj. 8, TV)
9 a (obj. 8, TV)

Culture Bearers

SOCIOLOGICAL PERSPECTIVE

Almost everything that you do—how you speak, what you eat, the kind of clothing you wear, how you define friendliness—is influenced by culture. Exposure to culture begins in the family as you learn all of the "what's" and "how to's" of human behavior. When you begin school, you are exposed to a much broader view of culture. You begin to learn a variety of ideas and ways of behaving. Throughout your life, you will continue to be influenced by various dimensions of culture, such as family, religion, social class, and geographic region. These and other factors are involved in the content of culture which society transmits to you.

Because you have learned from your family and society how and why to do or not to do certain things, you will tend to believe that your way is the natural way or the best way to do them. That is usual for people in all societies. But a study of other cultures reveals that although all people do certain things such as marry, cook food, play, work, and bury the dead, these things are done in ways that vary from one society to another, sometimes very noticeably.

By looking at our culture and the cultures of others, we become more aware of what influences our values and behavior. We come to understand ourselves and others more fully. The kind of human you are is largely determined by the kind of culture in which you learned your humanity.

LEARNING OBJECTIVES

Knowledge Objectives

1 Define culture.

2 Identify the elements of culture.

3 Identify the kinds of norms in a culture.

4 Identify several cultural universals.

5 Identify several variations within a culture.

6 Define and illustrate ethnocentrism.

7   Identify the major functions of culture.

8   Describe the process of cultural transmission.

9   Define cultural relativism.

10   Define and give an example of a subculture.

Attitudinal Objectives

1   Develop a better understanding of others' way of life by recognizing that their practices and beliefs are usually a realistic response to their situation.

2   Be aware of the extent to which our behavior is influenced by culture through the assumptions we make about values and behavior.

KEY TERMS

Culture   All of the shared elements in the way of life of a people, including values, beliefs, practices, and material objects.

Cultural universals   Behavior patterns and institutions which exist in all societies.

Cultural integration   The condition in which the various elements of a culture relate with consistency and harmony.

Subculture   A reasonably large number of people whose beliefs and practices vary noticeably from the dominant culture.

Norms   Rules or guidelines which serve as standards of behavior in a society.

Ethnocentrism   The tendency to believe that one's own race, religion, ethnic group, or region of the country is superior to others.

READING ASSIGNMENT

Robertson: *Sociology*, pp. 53–87

READING FOCUS QUESTIONS

1   What is the definition of culture?

2   What are the major elements of any culture?

3   Name the different kinds of norms which exist in all cultures.

4   What is meant by "cultural relativism"?

5   What is a subculture?

TV FOCUS QUESTIONS

1   Name several material and non-material items which culture includes.

2   What are some examples of cultural universals?

3   What is ethnocentrism? Give some examples.

4   What are the bases of variations within a culture?

5   How is culture transmitted from one generation to the next?

6   What purposes does culture serve?

OPTIONAL ACTIVITIES

1   Talk to a few friends or classmates about family rules and values when they were children and notice the beginnings of ethnocentrism as well as the transmission of standard cultural values.

2   Make a list of the rules which govern your daily activities. Note how many of these rules are taken-for-granted's upon which you have little influence.

POSTTEST

Multiple Choice

1   Culture is
   a. the material objects of a people.
   b. transmitted genetically.
   c. the shared beliefs and practices of a people.
   d. a and c.

2   The elements of culture include all *except*
   a. norms.
   b. beliefs.
   c. material objects.
   d. cities.

3   Norms include all *except*
   a. values and beliefs.
   b. customs and folkways.
   c. mores.
   d. a and c.

4 Cultural universals are illustrated by
   a. marrying and having children.
   b. working and burying the dead.
   c. sleeping in the bedroom and eating at a table.
   d. a and b.

5 Variations *within* a culture are often based upon
   a. religion and ethnicity.
   b. social class.
   c. geographic region.
   d. a and b.
   e. all of these.

6 Ethnocentrism is
   a. the belief that "our way is the best way."
   b. based primarily in the family.
   c. unique to Americans.
   d. a and b.
   e. all of these.

7 Which of the following best describes the purpose of culture?
   a. Culture controls individuals.
   b. Culture makes it possible for people to be different.
   c. Culture integrates individuals into society.
   d. a and b.

8 Which of these is *not* relevant to the transmission of culture?
   a. genetics.
   b. family life.
   c. language.
   d. symbols and material objects.

9 The recognition that one culture cannot be judged by the standards of another culture is called
   a. cultural relativism.
   b. cultural conflict.
   c. cultural variations.
   d. cultural integration.

10 The best example of an American subculture is
   a. housewives.
   b. high school students.
   c. homosexuals.
   d. Protestants.

POSTTEST ANSWERS

1 d (obj. 1, Text, p. 55)
2 d (obj. 2, Text, p. 62)
3 a (obj. 3, Text, p. 62)
4 d (obj. 4, Text, p. 72)
5 e (obj. 5, Text, p. 74)
6 a (obj. 6, Text, p. 72)
7 c (obj. 7, Text, p. 60)
8 a (obj. 8, Text, p. 60)
9 a (obj. 9, Text, p. 74)
10 c (obj. 10, Text, p. 76)

U.S. Culture

SOCIOLOGICAL PERSPECTIVE

In this lesson we will look first at a few obvious, highly visible ways in which most Americans are alike. These will be characteristics of U.S. culture which are most quickly seen by a foreign visitor and which are readily taken for granted by most Americans. We will examine briefly the effects of these visible characteristics upon our values and behavior. Then we will look more closely and analytically at basic American values—at what really makes us tick. We will examine the cultural themes which have been woven into our society since its beginning. We will also note some ways in which these themes have changed through our history and how those changes have affected our behavior.

LEARNING OBJECTIVES

Knowledge Objectives

1 Describe several surface characteristics of American culture.

2 Identify and describe several major themes or values in traditional American culture.

3 Identify and describe various factors which have given rise to these cultural values.

4 Identify and describe certain changes which have occurred in American culture in the past few decades, as well as the sources of those changes.

5 Describe the effect of the pleasure syndrome upon individual and group behavior.

Attitudinal Objectives

1 Develop a greater awareness and appreciation of some especially significant features of American culture.

2 Develop a greater awareness of the ways in which certain cultural themes or values affect the behavior of individuals and groups.

KEY TERMS

Cultural themes   Ideas or values which are identifiable throughout a society over time, expressing what is most important to that society.

Hedonism   A classic philosophy of or viewpoint on life which sees pleasure as the supreme good.

READING ASSIGNMENT

Additional Reading, "American Cultural Values"
Robertson: *Sociology*, pp. 64–67

READING FOCUS QUESTIONS

1   What are the most obvious characteristics of American society?

2   What are some effects of these characteristics upon our behavior?

3   What is the history of success as a cultural theme in the United States?

4   How do Americans feel about freedom?

5   How has the American attitude toward youth changed in the past half century?

6   What is the behavioral significance of our fascination with science and technology?

7   What is the contradiction in our love affair with large organizations?

TV FOCUS QUESTIONS

1   What are the surface or obvious characteristics of American culture?

2   What are the most important three or four cultural themes in America?

3   What is the cultural theme which has emerged in recent decades as the most noticeable in American society?

4   What factors contribute to the rise of the pleasure syndrome?

5   What are some of the effects of pleasure-seeking upon behavior?

OPTIONAL ACTIVITIES

1   Make a list of the five most important values in your life. Compare them with the values or themes discussed in this lesson.

2   Ask five people under 30 and five people over 50 to make such a list. Do some comparisons between those lists and with your own list.

POSTTEST

Multiple Choice

1 One of the most obvious characteristics of American culture is
   a. a fascination with technology.
   b. concern for tradition.
   c. economizing of natural resources.
   d. rejection of the pleasure principle.

2 As an American cultural theme, success has
   a. recently emerged as dominant.
   b. been significant since World War II.
   c. related only to material goods.
   d. long been dominant

3 A major factor contributing to the dominance of the success theme is
   a. the religious system.
   b. the political system.
   c. natural resources and climate.
   d. all of these.

4 The rise of the pleasure syndrome in recent decades seems related to
   a. the growth of religion.
   b. an increase in affluence and individualism.
   c. an increase in community involvement.
   d. a growing concern with family life.

5 The growth of the pleasure theme in American society has contributed to
   a. greater family and community solidarity.
   b. reduction in suicide, divorce, and crime.
   c. increased individualism and self interest.
   d. a greater sense of responsibility toward various groups.

6 The increased preoccupation which many Americans have with pleasure
   is most closely related to
   a. individual choices.
   b. the loss of religious influence.
   c. the loss of family ties.
   d. broad changes in the total social structure.

7 American society's preoccupation with youth is a phenomenon which
   a. is historic.
   b. began shortly after World War II.
   c. rose in the 1960's with the flower children.
   d. was stimulated mostly by "Year of the Child" activities.

POSTTEST ANSWERS

1 a (obj. 1, TV, Additional Reading)
2 d (obj. 2, TV)
3 d (obj. 3, TV, Additional Reading)
4 b (obj. 4, TV, Additional Reading)
5 c (obj. 4, 5, TV, Additional Reading)
6 d (obj. 5, TV, Additional Reading)
7 b (obj. 4, TV, Additional Reading)

American Cultural Values

An outsider, a stranger-first-time-visitor to our society would immediately observe some surface characteristics of our culture.

We are in love with technology—computers, calculators, video tape recorders, kidney dialysis machines, telestar, space vehicles, the latest auto model, pay-by-phone bank accounts, learn-by-TV college courses, automatic this and that. Digital clocks are in alarms, on the front of TV sets, in auto dashes, and on the wrists of millions of Americans. A watch one inch square and three-eights inch thick keeps time to the second, clocks a race to the 100th of a second, shows the day and date and alarms every 24 hours without resetting. Some even read out a calendar to the year 2000. The electronic space age brings color, complexity, speed, comfort, pleasure, and relief from boredom to many of us in many ways. Our fascination and involvement with technology reveal many things about our values which have created this technology. The technology, once created and embraced in daily life, in turn creates new values and affects human behavior in various ways. One simple example: although it may not change the promptness with which one keeps an appointment, the digital watch changes the way one perceives time, and one's consciousness of time as a precise measurement of a day. No longer is it "half past six" or "a quarter to seven." It is 6:30 or 6:45 or more likely 6:32 or 6:48. We've come a long way from telling time by the sun on the farm and from locating the big and the little hand on the clock dial. Time-conscious almost to an extreme for many years, Americans are becoming even more time-conscious with the digital watch and its alarm function. More people than ever are hearing beeps at pre-set intervals to disengage them from some activity or conversation and start another.

We are in love with pleasure—comfort in cars, houses, clothing; enjoyment of food, wine, music; excitement in sex, sports, movies, interpersonal relationships. There is an emphasis upon the good life unequalled since the days of Roman Emperors. This is caused and aided by affluence, advertising, anonymity, loneliness, lack of purpose and direction in life, and, boredom. Ask people why they disco every Friday night, why they watch violent movies, what pro football means to them, why they favor liberal sex standards. The level of individualism present in contemporary America is such that people's involvement is often with themselves and their individual needs and pleasures and less with small groups such as family, friends, neighbors, churches. This preoccupation with self isolates one from concerns about others, from pursuits which may be fulfilling. The individual ends up seeking pleasure, excitement and new experiences to fill his needs. There is no free land in the West, no gold to seek in the Hills, no frontier to challenge the restless ones. There is urbanism, smog, traffic, bureaucracy, and loneliness. Our society encourages the pursuit of pleasure through advertising, television programming, and the approval of hedonistic life styles.

We are a throw-away society. Whether one studies used beer cans or automobile junkyards, last year's spring suit or this summer's bikini, one sees that we are in love with change. We are in a hurry to get our food. We are insecure about looking good in the latest fashions. And we are customers and victims for the waste and exploitation of organizations, from giant corporations to the local massage parlor. The volume of trash unloaded daily in urban garbage dumps is staggering. Not only are we a throw-away society, but we wrap what we throw away in excessive material which also must be thrown away. We also throw away people and relationships—not, of course, in the literal sense ("Into which trash can would you like to be thrown?"), but in the sense of rather easily discarding relationships. The high divorce rate and the ease of divorce illustrate this point. We also find ourselves changing jobs, residences, clubs, and restaurants with relative ease. This fits into the cultural picture of a low pain threshold and a high expectation of life satisfaction which combine to limit our commitment to people and our patience with problems in human relationships.

These highly visible characteristics which indicate our love affair with technology, our pursuit of pleasure, and the throw-away syndrome, grow out of our values and needs and in turn create other values and needs. Industrialization requires growing technology. Affluence makes pleasure possible. A rapidly moving, urban society needs objects which can be used efficiently and not valued for themselves. So we develop computers, go with gusto on weekends, and change suits and cars every fall. How does all this affect our values and behavior? It helps us move faster, become more pleasure-oriented, and feel less responsibility for material objects, including those of other people. It forces us to face more choices and deal with more alternatives in values and lifestyles. The proliferation of options reduces the proportion of one's daily life which is guided by tradition, and increases the portion which is subject to decision and change, or perhaps indecision and uncertainty.

Now that our visitor/stranger has observed some obvious and interesting features of American society, let us ask him to look more closely at values which underlie these interesting features: values which are shared by most Americans as cultural goals. That is, items, concepts or behavior patterns to which they aspire, even though many do not achieve these goals.

A dominant theme in U.S. culture is success. It is also known as work, the Protestant Ethic, individual achievement. Various elements have combined to create an environment favorable to high success motivation in the United States from its early days to the present. Ecologically, it is a rich nation: climate, soil, mineral resources, water. Politically, it has been and still is the most open society of modern times in terms of civil liberties, individual rights, and an open class system. Examples of this are freedom of movement, residence, investment, profit-taking.

Morally, or religiously, the nation has, through what came to be known as the Protestant Ethic, encouraged individual effort and success. Its "Hitch your wagon to a star," and "He who gets there first with the most" attitudes have encouraged risk-taking and perseverance toward individual success. The earliest Americans from Europe were Protestants. Many of them believed in John Calvin's teaching of the elect: the doctrine which held that some are saved eternally and that some are lost.

This doctrine held that only God knew who was among the elect and He would not tell anyone. However, it held that well accomplished work was a sign of God's grace. The open social structure of the new country held promise and opportunity for upward mobility. It became, therefore, a matter of "work like the devil to beat the devil." Success became the primary measure of self-worth for Americans. The individualism of American culture found its fullest expression in occupational competition. We enjoy rags-to-riches stories. We like the idea that if one works hard enough long enough he will succeed. We enjoy the comfort of blaming individuals for their failures rather than admitting that something might be wrong in the system. And many Americans do indeed find self-worth in their success, although others suffer with a sense of personal inadequacy, undoubtedly heightened by our cultural emphasis on everyone being highly successful.

Another major cultural value is freedom, closely associated with such concepts as equality, democracy, and individualism. These are words and concepts which most Americans learn in the first grade. We think of freedom as freedom from police-state-like external controls. We think of freedom to live, work, move about when and where we please; freedom to marry, divorce, to have or not have children; to associate or not associate with people; to worship or not worship as we choose. Americans' historic concept of freedom relates negatively to government. Primarily, the government is seen as functioning to guarantee freedom—not running our lives by telling us with whom we eat, sleep, go to church or school, or live by. Whether one thinks of gun control, abortion, racial integration, affirmative action, or other issues which have government attention or intervention, many Americans resent many aspects of the government's actions and consider them infringements upon individual rights.

Some rights are constitutional—the right of assembly, the right to bear arms, the freedom of press. Other rights are grass-roots, common sense, taken-for-granted because nobody ever questioned them before. In the early 1970's, state police rang doorbells in a northern state to check heating thermostats in private residences for compliance with federal energy requests. A decades-long national effort to build high speed interstate highways came near its completion only to coincide with energy problems and simplistic solutions such as the 55 mph speed limit. As the bumper stickers say, we can live with that law. We can also live with other laws or regulations which may or may not be cost-effective or energy efficient but which are imposed by a federal bureaucracy which few Americans trust and even fewer believe is competent to make decisions which affect significantly their freedoms and daily activities. Americans value freedom. Just how much they will sacrifice for that freedom in terms of comfort, security, and material success is unknown. Until recently, challenges to freedom were international in scope and settled by wars. They were local and settled by whatever means available. Freedom is a complex value—which freedoms are desired and at what cost of other freedoms? Apathy in local and national elections; distrust of government, of particular segments of industry, of political and religious leaders; and frustration in the face of rising challenges to individual freedoms all must be considered when Americans' value of freedom is discussed. Another important variable is the responsibility of society, government, someone, to protect the rights and welfare of the weak and underprivil ged in society.

Equality is a complex concept for Americans. On the one hand, they take pride in being average, just-as-good-as-anyone-else individuals, and in speaking up for a fair shake for everyone regardless of color, creed, or age. On the other hand, the competition for success is so stiff that once out of the starting gate, Americans tend to run an "every man for himself" race without much regard for slow or lame horses. Most of them tend to believe that they have what they have because they worked hard for it (which is, in many cases, quite true) and that others do not have much because they don't deserve it.

Democracy is a near synonym in American thought for equality. It means that everyone gets his vote, his day in court, his even chance. But there are power, pressure, and interest groups of many kinds which interfere with the smooth functioning of the democratic system. There are lobby groups in Washington and city hall. There are prejudicial attitudes and discriminatory acts which contradict the values of equality and democracy. The same organizations which served and still serve useful purposes also hinder equality. Medical associations, labor unions, educational associations, neighborhood associations and many others have a mixed effect upon freedom, equality, and democracy.

One of the most obvious cultural values in the United States is materialism, with associated ideas about pleasure, leisure, and casual living. This group of related values or themes was noted earlier as part of the view available to our alien visitor. A closer look reinforces the idea that Americans are indeed committed to these values. The amount of time spent relaxing, the insistence upon casual dress and fast-food service, microwave ovens, remote control televisions, automatic climate control autos, resorts, sports, "gusto" situations all attest to our preoccupation with these values.

Until the post-World War II period in American cultural development, there was little emphasis upon youth. Of course families loved their children, but it was hardly "year of the child." In rural America, children were an economic asset. That reality, coupled with low birth control technology and certain religious dogma created a high birth rate. By 1950, the country was sufficiently urbanized that children were not needed in the labor force. However, the growing middle class and the increased affluence of Everyman turned his attention to the fascination of having large families. Many decided about then to raise their own basketball team. The baby boom of 1947 got it started; the rising affluence continued it. As the war baby cohorts moved through various life cycles—diaper stage, first toys stage, kindergarten, first grade, high school—they had incredible impact upon technology, education, production, sales, housing, records, cars, clothing, and almost every other aspect of American life. We became a child-obsessed culture. By the late 1960's and early 1970's there were so many college-aged youth with so much freedom and affluence that the adult culture could not effectively contain them in the usual ways.

Other concerns we may have about youth include their status in education, part-time work, religion, and family. Traditional rules of "teacher is in charge here" have been challenged by street bullies and by federal courts. Students' rights, due process, society-wide arguments have all come down rather heavily upon traditional classroom, athletic field, and maltshop scenes.

At the heart of an increasingly complex American value system is the value known variously as religion, morality, or humanitarianism. Early American Indians were heavily influenced by their concepts of deity. The first immigrants were religious. There seems to be a resurgence of interest and activity in religious matters today. At the heart of our morality lie such beliefs as the value of the individual, the right to independence and freedom, and equal opportunity to seek success and happiness. As with other cultural values, religion is complex. Its teachings are used to justify racism and to oppose racism. Its values vary from human rights for all to mystical concerns available only to the initiated.

Part of American idealism involves the right to work. Another part involves the responsibility to work or not eat—a biblical injunction variously interpreted. Thus, in the face of a traditional American humanitarianism toward people in need, there are conflicting ideas about welfare. We tend to see assistance to victims of flood, fire, or other catastrophes as emergency, temporary assistance, to be followed by individual responsibility for one's own long term recovery. Most Americans are not bothered significantly by economic inequalities suffered by others. Their religion not only does not inhibit this comfort, it often fits into the rationale which justifies or explains it.

Americans value efficiency and innovation. They reward builders of better mousetraps—and cars, refrigerators, socket wrenches, television sets, cameras, and typewriters. Doing it better, getting ahead of the other guy, doing the best one can, all contribute to the way of life Americans consider the best. In addition, many Americans believe that science can, and will, eventually do anything. It got man to the moon and back, created telestar, computers, and instant replay. It will also cure cancer, replace worn out body parts, and solve the energy crisis.

The major significance of this trust in science and technology seems to be an attitude of insistence upon quick solutions, an unwillingness to accept defeat. "Fix it now." "Get an expert." Once children merely died of dread diseases, or premature births. Now we have ICU's for preemies, specialists to care only for them, blood changes, and diagnostic equipment. A child loses an arm in an accident. A team of surgeons spends 10 hours reattaching the arm—and it works! A tired heart is replaced or piggy-backed or revalved—and it works! We become accustomed to technological miracles and are less willing to accept stoically the inevitability of death or disability. With the existence of long-distance computer hookups, Concorde flights, artificial organs, our expectations of science grows—as do concerns about ethics, legalities, and moral issues relating to new possibilities and practices.

In a sense contradictory to the American spirit of individualism is the attitude that if something needs to be done, an organization can be formed to do it. It may be a neighborhood committee or an international conglomerate, but Americans are highly organized. Organizations can be non-profit, human value oriented, such as churches, scout troops, Great Books Clubs or city symphonies, or profit oriented such as IBM, GM, AT & T or the local chain of pizza parlors or bowling alleys.

Most Americans, except for those in the lower class, belong to numerous organizations of many types and sub-types: church, union, professional organization, sports league, political organization, civic club, book club. These serve various purposes: economic gain or security, leisure time consumption, emotional, psychological or moral support, power accumulation. They are often interest groups which come into conflict with each other. Membership may involve a minimal commitment of money and effort or a great deal of personal dedication. Because U.S. culture has become so urban, mass, and heterogeneous, many Americans join groups to find identity, friendship, and power.

Americans are like all people in some ways. In other ways we are unique or at least far down the continuum from other cultures. Some elements of our culture are especially symbolic: movies, baseball, Thanksgiving, hamburgers, Coke, Chevrolet. Some behavorial or personality patterns are American: friendliness, independence, competitiveness, humanitarianism, violence. We all grow up in the midst of these elements, taking them for granted as the right way, the best way, or perhaps the only way to live. We are told to stand up straight, brush our teeth well, salute the flag, say "sir" to teachers and policemen, go to school, get a job, marry, be successful. While there are certainly variations on these themes and there are people who do not do some of these things, most people do in fact follow cultural dictates rather closely. It is these cultural themes which become our "given's" for attitudes, behavior, and expectations of ourselves and of others. While American choices are much wider and less traditional and limited than those of many other cultures, they are nonetheless the major limiting factor in our behavior.

What is an American? What does he believe? Whatever he is and whatever he believes, and however strange or wonderful or terrible all that is to our alien visitor observing American culture, he is just that: American born, taught, and acclimated; molded by the values of freedom, work, and religion; and, more recently, subject to the increased influences of materialism, science, and complex organization.

4

Becoming Human

SOCIOLOGICAL PERSPECTIVE

In the late 1970's, a lot of interest was generated by a process known as cloning—the reproduction of physical organisms such as frogs or humans by a process involving cell manipulation. The idea is to produce superior beings and reduce physical defects and intellectual limitations. A major concern about the process centers on the reality that most of what we think of as "human" does not come from biology, but from the social environment. That is, human individuals learn to think, feel, reason, choose, and behave.

That which we value most about ourselves and others around us arises from the complex interaction among human individuals involving language, values, and shared experiences. Our humanness is something which begins with the first interaction after birth and continues throughout life. It is, paradoxically, fragile and enduring, unique and universal, present early in life and yet changing significantly throughout life.

In this lesson we will study the social origin of humanness, the vital role of language, and some variations in how what individuals learn about themselves affects their life. This lesson is about the process of socialization, how individuals learn what they need to be humans, to function in human society.

LEARNING OBJECTIVES

Knowledge Objectives

1 Define socialization.

2 Explain the influence of biology and environment upon individual development.

3 Explain the effects of severe isolation in early childhood.

4 Discuss the importance of language in the socialization process.

5 Define self.

6 Explain the concept of "looking glass self."

7 Give an example of defective socialization and one of effective
   socialization.

Attitudinal Objectives

1 Understand and appreciate more fully the source and nature of
   humanness.

2 Become more aware of and show greater understanding of some reasons
   why some individuals do not function well in society.

KEY TERMS

Socialization The process by which society transmits to an individual the
physical, mental, and social skills needed to become human and participate
in society.

Self An individual's awareness of being a distinct, separate being with
identity and uniqueness.

Looking glass self Cooley's concept of the way awareness of individual
identity arises through reading the impressions others have of us.

Symbolic interaction Interaction between humans which involves the use
of symbols such as language and gestures.

READING ASSIGNMENT

Robertson: *Sociology*, pp. 77–79, 115–128

READING FOCUS QUESTIONS

1 What is socialization?

2 What is the difference between "nature" and "nurture?"

3 What are some effects upon children reared in extreme isolation?

4 What is the self?

5 What is the looking glass self?

6 What is symbolic interaction?

TV FOCUS QUESTIONS

1 What is "being human?"

2 What are some effects of severe isolation upon children?

3 What is the role of nature in developing humanness?

4 What is the role of nurture in developing humanness?

5 What is socialization?

6 What is the self?

7 What is the looking glass self?

8 What is the role of language in the socialization process?

9 What are some examples of good and bad socialization?

OPTIONAL ACTIVITIES

1 Visit a school or class in special education and observe the behavior of young children with some form of severe limitation upon their learning ability. How does this behavior affect their acceptance by others as being fully human?

2 Make a list of the five most important values or beliefs you have and see if you can determine their origin in your life.

POSTTEST

True–False

1 Socialization is the process ending in early childhood by which individuals learn to be human.

2 Although the debate rages on, it is now essentially clear that nature has greater influence upon individuals than nurture.

3 Most children reared in extreme isolation recover completely from its effects if the treatment is proper.

4 Each person possesses a self at birth and it remains essentially unchanged throughout life.

5 Language is the most important variable in the socialization process.

6 The looking-glass self is Cooley's concept of how one's view of self comes from others' responses to one.

7 "Hi, I'm five. I'm pretty" is an example of a strong self-image in spite of defective socialization.

8 Although social contact is helpful, a person can form a sense of self without it.

POSTTEST ANSWERS

1 F (obj. 1, TV, Text, p. 115)
2 F (obj. 2, TV, Text, p. 117)
3 F (obj. 3, TV, Text, p. 120)
4 F (obj. 5, TV, Text, p. 122)
5 T (obj. 4, TV, Text, p. 77)
6 T (obj. 6, TV, Text, p. 122)
7 F (obj. 8, TV)
8 F (obj. 5, TV, Text, p. 120)

Childhood Socialization: Television

SOCIOLOGICAL PERSPECTIVE

How much television did you watch as a child? Did it affect the kind of person you have become? How important is the role of television in socializing children today?

Socialization has been defined as the process through which an individual becomes human. It is the learning of skills, values, attitudes, and behavior patterns a person needs to participate in society. The major social agencies which are involved in the process are the family, peer group, and school.

In recent years, the influence of television upon the socialization of children has been examined by social scientists. Most children are exposed to many hours of television, watching all kinds of programs and being given information about many aspects of life and many views of life not otherwise available to them.

There is often a complex relationship between various socializing agencies. A child is told one thing by his parents about fighting with other children. There is a different version by a teacher, another by a group of friends, and perhaps yet a fourth is depicted on television. It would be rare indeed if all four versions agreed.

After noting the role of traditional agencies in the socialization process, this lesson gives special attention to the role of television. Just how extensive is its impact upon the learning and behavior of children? In what areas does it have noticeable influence? Who should be responsible for managing this important dimension of socialization?

LEARNING OBJECTIVES

Knowledge Objectives

1 Identify various agencies of socialization in childhood.

2 Describe the role of media in the socialization process.

3 Describe the major influence of the family upon children.

4 Describe the major influence of the school upon children.

5 Describe the role of the peer group in childhood socialization.

6   Identify several ways in which television affects the process of socialization in childhood.

Attitudinal Objectives

1   Understand and appreciate the complexity of the relationships among various agencies of socialization.

2   Become more aware of the influence of television upon the socialization of children and appreciate the seriousness of the responsibility of monitoring that influence.

KEY TERMS

Agency of socialization   An institution such as a family or school, or other structured situation, by which the content of culture is transmitted to individuals.

Peer group   A number of individuals of approximately the same age or interest who interact frequently and have influence upon each other.

READING ASSIGNMENT

Robertson: *Sociology*, pp. 128–131

READING FOCUS QUESTIONS

1   What are agencies of socialization?

2   What is the role of the family in early socialization?

3   What is the role of the school in early socialization?

4   How does the peer group function in early socialization?

5   How extensive is the influence of television as a socializing influence upon children?

TV FOCUS QUESTIONS

1   What are the major traditional agencies of socialization in childhood?

2   What is one major function of each of these agencies?

3   How extensive is the involvement of the typical child with television?

4   What kinds of programs do children watch?

5 Name three ways in which television has a problematic or negative effect upon children?

OPTIONAL ACTIVITIES

1 Ask ten children under eight years of age which television shows they watch and which are their favorites. See if you can determine how many hours a week they watch television.

2 Examine a television schedule and list the programs which are most likely to be viewed by children (after school, early evening, and weekends). Note the type of programs and the content, then observe the proportion of programming designed for children.

3 Ask ten sets of parents if they control the amount and kind of television programs their children watch. Are their concerns about the type of programming, the amount of time or what?

POSTTEST

True–False

1 The major agencies of socialization in children are church, school, and family.

2 The earliest and most important influence upon children is the peer group.

3 The widespread influence of television in the past two decades has made it the only type of mass media with very much influence upon children.

4 A major importance of family socialization is that first close emotional ties are established there.

5 The family has the greatest impact of all agencies in early childhood.

6 School aids in preparing children for later life in that it judges them by more general standards of performance, beauty, and intelligence than the family or peer groups.

7 Peer groups loosen family ties and compete strongly for a child's loyalty in very early life.

8 Some recent studies indicate that children watch television from one to 72 hours a week and average about 23 hours a week.

9 Studies indicate that television increases a child's imagination.

10 Contrary to popular opinion, heavy doses of television programs containing aggressive behavior do not increase violence in children.

POSTTEST ANSWERS

1 F (obj. 1, TV, Text, p. 129)
2 F (obj. 1, TV, Text, p. 128)
3 F (obj. 2, TV, Text, p. 130)
4 T (obj. 3, TV, Text, p. 128)
5 T (obj. 3, TV)
6 T (obj. 4, TV, Text, p. 129)
7 F (obj. 5, TV)
8 T (obj. 6, TV)
9 F (obj. 6, TV)
10 F (obj. 6, TV)

Sex Roles

6

SOCIOLOGICAL PERSPECTIVE

At the moment of birth, society labels a child by sex. In U.S. culture, as in other world cultures, the celebration tends to be more enthusiastic at the birth of a male child than at that of a female child. Male children are often valued more highly. They are heads of families, workers, providers, warriors, planners, thinkers; and they continue the lineage. It would not be unusual in some societies to find a father who has a standing offer of $1,000 for the married child who produces the first grandson. Or, if he is an empire builder, the offer may include the empire.

In this lesson we will study the social forces and the cultural definitions and expectations which determine the content of sexual identity and behavior. We will also see some ways individuals are socialized into sexual identities and sexual behavior through their relationships within the family, the school, the peer group, the work group, and other groups of various kinds.

Many questions will be examined during the course of this lesson. How is sex defined? What is masculine? What is feminine? What are the origins of these definitions and expectations? What are some of the consequences of sexual identification? To what extent are differences between males and females biological? To what extent are they culturally imposed? What are some myths in the common male and female stereotypes?

LEARNING OBJECTIVES

Knowledge Objectives

1 Define sex, sex gender, and sex role.

2 Identify some myths about sex roles which exist in U.S. culture.

3 Contrast the functional and conflict theories of sex roles.

4 Identify cultural expectations relating to masculine and feminine personality and behavior.

5 Identify actual differences between males and females.

6   Identify the basic causes for sex role differences.

7   Identify certain tasks in the division of labor which are almost always done by men, almost always done by women, and others which are done by both men and women.

8   Describe the influence of family, school, and peer groups on the development of sex roles.

9   Describe the influence of media on sex roles.

10   Describe changes occurring in sex roles in the United States.

Attitudinal Objectives

1   Develop a greater awareness of the nature and sources of sex roles and a greater appreciation of one's own experiences in this regard, as well as those of others.

2   Develop a greater awareness and appreciation of the diversity of sex roles in a cross-cultural context and thus greater respect and tolerance for individuals or societies whose cultural definitions of sex roles differ from ours.

KEY TERMS

Sex   A biological category of male or female.

Sex gender   Cultural concepts of masculinity or femininity which create the psychological awareness one has of one's own sexuality.

Sex roles   Learned patterns of masculine and feminine behavior based upon societal expectations.

READING ASSIGNMENT

Robertson: *Sociology,* pp. 313–331

READING FOCUS QUESTIONS

1   What biological evidence is there that differences exist between males and females?

2   What psychological evidence is there that differences exist between males and females?

3   What cross-cultural evidence is there that differences exist between males and females?

4   What is the basis of sexist ideology in western culture?

TV FOCUS QUESTIONS

1. What are the three basic ways in which sex is identified?

2. What are some of the myths and assumptions about sex gender in U.S. culture?

3. What are some real intellectual differences between males and females?

4. What are some real behavioral differences between males and females?

5. What are the basic causes for sex role differences?

6. How do men and women divide the labor in various cultures?

7. What are the sources of influence upon sex role development?

OPTIONAL ACTIVITIES

1. Ask five males and five females of approximately the same age what males and females are supposed to do in the work world. Compare their answers.

2. Watch any five one-hour television programs on any network and list the jobs held by male characters and female characters. Compare the prestige, authority, and responsibility involved in the jobs.

POSTTEST

True–False

 1. The difference between sex gender and sex role is that one is biological and the other is cultural.

 2. One of the myths in U.S. culture which is reasonably accurate holds that men are rational and aggressive and women are emotional and passive.

3. The conflict theory of sex roles holds that it is natural for males and females to experience conflict.

 4. American culture portrays the ideal woman as gentle, compassionate, and sexy and the ideal man as confident, aggressive, and in control of his emotions.

 5. In terms of average differences, boys are better than girls in math and girls have higher verbal ability.

 6. The two basic causes of sex role differences are biology and culture.

 7. In cultures all around the world, men usually make weapons and hunt and women usually cook, tend the fires, and do the heavy work.

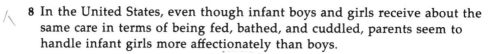

8 In the United States, even though infant boys and girls receive about the same care in terms of being fed, bathed, and cuddled, parents seem to handle infant girls more affectionately than boys.

9 Media in the United States typically portray males and females as having equal ability, similar psychological traits, and similar behavioral patterns.

10 In spite of the influence of ERA, the increase of women in the work force, and the rise of the educational level of women, there has been little noticeable change in sex roles in the United States in the past decade.

POSTTEST ANSWERS

1 F (obj. 1, TV)
2 F (obj. 2, TV)
3 F (obj. 3, Text, p. 319)
4 T (obj. 4, TV)
5 T (obj. 5, TV)
6 T (obj. 6, TV)
7 T (obj. 7, TV, Text, p. 317)
8 T (obj. 8, TV)
9 F (obj. 9, TV)
10 F (obj. 10, TV, Text, p. 323)

The Life Cycle: Aging

SOCIOLOGICAL PERSPECTIVE

Socialization is the process by which society teaches the individual how to think, behave, and feel in order to be effective and accepted in the society. It enables the individual to be social, that is, to create and maintain relationships with people and groups. The socialization process is lifelong—at least, it lasts until the individual is no longer facing new situations, learning new things, or entering new relationships.

In this lesson we will be looking at adult socialization, the process by which society continues to teach individuals how to act after they become adults. By the time adulthood is reached, primary socialization has been largely completed. The individual has an image of self, some understanding of and commitment to the norms and values of society, and a basic grasp of skills necessary to function as an adult.

There are a number of socializing experiences which most adults face: entering the work force, taking one's own apartment, getting married, having a child, moving to a new community (or nation), getting a divorce, being promoted on the job. All of these involve learning about new responsibilities, expectations, rewards, and behavior patterns.

The socialization of adults differs significantly from that of children and adolescents. First, the content of socialization is different. Children are learning the most basic elements of human behavior and values—love, warmth, security, up, down, right, wrong—the very fundamental knowledge and attitudes necessary to be human and to get along in society. Adults learn job skills, parenting roles, and special behaviors required in certain adult roles. Second, the socialization of adults is more voluntary than that of children and adolescents. Adults are more likely to understand the reasons for their new learning and thus to be more highly motivated than children. They choose a number of their new roles, such as marriage, college, religion, or job. Thus their participation in the socialization process is likely to be more cooperative and active.

The mature adult role is difficult to learn in U.S. culture. The culture is complex. Adult roles from which one can choose are many and varied. The avenue to successful adulthood is open to a number of variations. One may drop out of high school, or finish college, or enter graduate school. He may take a job in a large corporation, start his own business, or do both. The absence of strong tradition and the presence of many channels to adult success create some confusion for adults. Even the age at which one becomes an adult is flexible in the United States. Some assume the role successfully by dropping out of high school and taking adult jobs. Others' full acceptance into adulthood may be delayed for several years if they stay in school or do not have a full-time job.

Adult socialization is continuing for life, is highly variable, and focuses upon practical matters. In the United States and other advanced societies, it is highly complex and poses many problematic decisions and experiences for most adults.

One of the more interesting and important aspects of the adult life cycle is that of aging. Until recent years, little serious attention had been given to the study of aging, or gerontology. This lesson takes a careful look at the physical and social aspects of aging and at the need for improving the process of socializing Americans for being older. It also examines various modes of behavior adapted by individuals as they grow older, as well as their feelings about being older.

LEARNING OBJECTIVES

Knowledge Objectives

1 Define adult life cycle and describe the stages.

2 Define resocialization and give some examples.

3 Describe some failures of the socialization process.

4 Describe some physical and social aspects of aging.

5 Define ageism.

6 Describe different modes of adaptation to growing older.

7 Describe the effects of ageism on the total society.

Attitudinal Objectives

1 Become more aware of and appreciate more fully the nature of the aging process and its influence upon individuals and society.

2 Become more sensitive to the realities facing older people and to the probability of our facing the same realities.

KEY TERMS

Gerontology   The scientific study of aging.

Life cycle   The sequence of stages through which individuals pass from birth until death.

Resocialization   Learning which takes place when individuals face new situations or conditions which require revision of values and behavior patterns.

Ageism   A set of concepts, usually negative stereotypes, which relates to the condition of older people.

READING ASSIGNMENT

Robertson: *Sociology*, pp. 131–137, 331–343

READING FOCUS QUESTIONS

1   What are some types of socialization?

2   What is the life cycle?

3   What are some failures of the socialization process?

4   What does recent research indicate about the value of more open discussions of death?

TV FOCUS QUESTIONS

1   What constitutes the human life cycle?

2   What is a rite of passage?

3   What is the most serious flaw in the American socialization process?

4   What is the "graying of America?"

5   What are some biological effects of growing older?

6   What are some social effects of growing older?

7   What is ageism?

8   How do various older people adapt to growing older?

9   How does failure to understand aging affect society as a whole?

OPTIONAL ACTIVITIES

1   Write your age on a sheet of paper. Beginning at age ten, and using ten year intervals, write a sentence description of what you were doing and expect to be doing at those intervals.

2   Visit a nursing home for older people. Observe conditions and activities. Talk with a few residents about their lives. Compare this experience with that of visiting an older couple in their residence.

POSTTEST

True–False

1   Socialization begins at birth and continues until maturity and the beginning of old age.

2   Resocialization involves learning that requires a sharp break with past attitudes and behavior patterns.

3   The socialization process is typically more practical and effective in simple societies than in modern, industrialized ones.

4   One of the life areas in which U.S. socialization functions most effectively is in preparation for old age.

5   Although aging is obviously physical in nature, there are also several very significant social dimensions to the process.

6   One problem with aging is ignorance of the actual emotional and social experiences of becoming older.

7   Although the popular stereotype of aging seems to center upon the nursing home scene, actually very few old people experience isolation.

8   Ageism, unlike other social stereotypes such as racism and sexism, actually has very few negative effects upon either older people or society.

9   Most older people adapt to their changed life conditions in very much the same way.

10   In spite of their efforts to remain active, many old people find that withdrawal from society is a common feature of life.

11   The treatment accorded older people is also a problem for the rest of society in that it causes others to expect the same treatment when they are old—and thus to fear growing old.

POSTTEST ANSWERS

1   F (obj. 1, TV)
2   T (obj. 2, Text, p. 131)

3 T (obj. 3, Text, p. 135)
4 F (obj. 3, Text, p. 136)
5 T (obj. 4, TV, Text, p. 136)
6 T (obj. 3, TV)
7 F (obj. 4, TV)
8 F (obj. 5, TV, Text, p. 335)
9 F (obj. 6, TV)
10 T (obj. 6, TV)
11 T (obj. 7, TV)

Social Groups and Norms

Groups and Social Organization

SOCIOLOGICAL PERSPECTIVE

Think of how much time you spend in activities which involve the presence of other individuals: work, play, school, worship, entertainment, politics. Almost everything which people do in these areas of living in our society, they do with at least one individual and often many other individuals.

This lesson takes a look at two of the most basic and important concepts in sociology: groups and social organization. A great portion of the subject matter of sociology involves human activity in groups of one kind or another. Most of our needs are met by our membership in groups of various kinds. The kinds of persons we become and what we think of ourselves depend greatly upon group memberships and identifications.

As you study this lesson, note carefully the definition of "group." It is not just any number of people who happen to be doing anything. Six people waiting on an elevator do not necessarily constitute a group—unless they are all members of the same family or a team planning to rob a bank. If the elevator sticks between floors for six hours, they will probably become a group, unless all of them faint immediately or become hysterical until they are rescued.

Groups are of many kinds and have many purposes. We may focus on a particular group, such as a family. But to understand fully all of the influences upon that group, we must examine its relationships with other groups in society. We must back off with wide-angle lenses and view the broad picture. A hitchhiker sees a single stretch of pavement going in two directions. An aerial view of a metropolitan freeway system reveals a quite different and more complex perspective. It shows many lines of pavement, intersections, exits—and it includes the connections which those elements make with parking lots, buildings, residences and shopping centers.

Human activity is also patterned or organized in particular ways. From the daily, routine, and repeated activities patterns emerge, whether we examine a family at dinner, a factory producing television sets or a wide receiver going out for a pass. Sociologists refer to these patterns as "social organization." The broader and more complex aspects of social organization involve how a society is organized into social classes, work groups, political parties, and how it manages all of its other functions. The way in which society is organized has a powerful influence upon human behavior, quality of life, and life chances. Understanding the existence and nature of these patterns is basic to the study of sociology.

A special note seems in order concerning the status of small, primary groups in American society today. Social, political, and economic conditions since World War II have made it increasingly difficult to create and maintain primary groups. Whether we consider family, community, church, work, or friendship groups, urbanization has had a startling effect upon them. Urban populations are more heterogeneous, diverse, mobile. They have differing interests, work schedules, life styles, and value systems. About the time one finds individuals of similar interests and schedules, they are transferred to another city, move across town or work a different shift. Some factors, such as the long-distance telephone and the ready jet flights have shrunk distance and kept long-term friendships intact. But these advantages are for the reasonably affluent and they do not substitute for the weekly six-hour bridge party or poker game.

When the development of a society destroys small groups or erects barriers to the maintenance of traditional small groups, some individuals find new kinds of small groups to join. They join Great Books Clubs, take tennis lessons, seek intimacy in bars, join Parents without Partners, and take cruises to Hawaii. They write Ann or Abbey, consult dating services, change jobs, religion, or residence. Many sociologists are optimistic about the resilience and ingenuity of individuals in finding some way to meet their need for membership in small groups. They insist that new forms and relationships emerge to replace the lost ones; the need is so pervasive that the search goes on.

On balance it seems that many individuals are experiencing increased difficulty in making connections which satisfy their needs of belonging and intimacy. Continuing high rates of depression, drug abuse, suicide, and other forms of extreme behavior indicate both individual and cultural failure. There is a large number of individuals in periods of transition in relationships, such as divorced individuals whose anticipated or eventual remarriage is delayed. More people are between jobs, in temporary jobs, halfway through school and not quite certain about their future.

A mixed-blessing condition seems to prevail in which options and possibilities are great but are accompanied by an extended period of uncertainty and possible confusion. As older, more traditional groups disappear, new groups come forth to take their place. But the form of the new groups and the rules by which they operate are as yet unclear.

LEARNING OBJECTIVES

Knowledge Objectives

1 Define social group.

2 Distinguish between primary and secondary groups.

3 Describe the importance of groups to individuals.

4 Discuss changes in the status of primary and secondary groups in recent American society.

5 Define social organization.

6 Discuss the importance of social organization to human behavior and life chances.

7 Define society.

8 Define status and role.

9 Define institution.

Attitudinal Objectives

1 Develop a greater awareness and appreciation of the multiplicity and influence of groups in your own life.

2 Develop a greater awareness of the effect of changes in your group memberships upon your attitudes and behavior.

KEY TERMS

Group   Two or more individuals with a sense of mutual identification based upon shared interaction and goals.

Primary group   A number of people, usually small, who interact with frequency, continuity, intimacy in face-to-face situations.

Secondary group   A number of people, small or large, who interact with some continuity and for instrumental purposes without intimacy or shared personal values.

Social organization   The patterning or structuring of relationships; the systematic, repeated features of human interaction.

Status   A position in society.

Role   Obligations and privileges of a status.

Institution   A stable and regularized way of meeting a basic social need.

Society   A group of interacting individuals sharing physical space and culture.

READING ASSIGNMENT

Robertson: *Sociology*, pp. 89–95, 101–112, 167–175

READING FOCUS QUESTIONS

1 What is the essence of a group?

2 What are the major distinctions between primary and secondary groups?

3 What is a reference group?

4 What determines whether a small group is primary or secondary?

5 What are some effects upon a group of changes in its size?

TV FOCUS QUESTIONS

1 What is the special meaning which sociologists give to "group"?

2 What are the two basic kinds of groups which sociologists study?

3 What is the importance of primary groups to the community?

4 How have primary groups and membership in them changed with the development of U.S. society?

5 How do people cope with the impersonality of secondary groups?

6 Define and give an example of social organization.

OPTIONAL ACTIVITIES

1 Make a list of all of the groups of which you are a member. Rank them in terms of their importance to you. Identify them as primary or secondary.

2 Keep a daily journal of your activities for one week. Note those which were repeated and the presence and influence of patterns in those activities.

POSTTEST

Multiple Choice

1 The best example of a group is six
   a. people waiting for an elevator.
   b. friends having pizza.
   c. people at an auto accident.
   d. patients in intensive care.

2 The major distinction between a primary and a secondary group is the
   a. purpose of the group.
   b. size of the group.
   c. value of the group.
   d. leadership of the group.

3 Groups are important to individuals because
   a. all human activity occurs in groups.
   b. groups control human activity completely.
   c. so much human activity takes place within and is influenced by groups.
   d. the most effective human efforts are in groups.

4 Primary groups in U.S. society have changed in recent years in that
   a. the need for primary groups is less vital.
   b. such groups as family, community, and friendship are affected adversely by social change.
   c. primary groups traditional to society are disappearing and no new ones are emerging to replace them.
   d. traditional primary groups are more stable than before.

5 Social organization is best illustrated by
   a. the Red Cross.
   b. IBM.
   c. the patterned activities of a family.
   d. a civic club in community service.

6 Social organization is important to individuals because it
   a. provides the social order necessary to conduct human affairs.
   b. gives people various choices in interaction.
   c. leaves individuals entirely free to behave as they wish.
   d. influences major issues and decisions.

7 A number of people constitute a society if they
   a. know each other at work or play.
   b. interact with shared values and space.
   c. have affection and respect for each other.
   d. have the same goals and rules.

8 The distinction between status and role is that
   a. one is social and the other is personal.
   b. one occupies a status and plays a role.
   c. one is ascribed and the other is achieved.
   d. one is more important as a social institution.

9 Which of these is an institution?
   a. Harvard University
   b. General Motors
   c. Red Cross
   d. Sports

POSTTEST ANSWERS

1 b (obj. 1, TV)
2 a (obj. 2, TV, Text, p. 93)
3 c (obj. 3, TV)
4 b (obj. 4, TV)
5 c (obj. 5, TV)
6 a (obj. 6, TV)

7 b (obj. 7, Text, p. 89)
8 b (obj. 8, Text, p. 91)
9 d (obj. 9, Text, p. 93)

Formal Organizations

j

SOCIOLOGICAL PERSPECTIVE

The next time you drive down an urban freeway or walk through a shopping mall, notice the dominance of large organizations in the scene: Sears, IBM, GM, CBS, NFL and hundreds of others. Formal organizations are powerful in every phase of human life: work, education, religion, medicine, sports, entertainment, politics, warfare. They have risen to meet the needs of large and complex populations.

This lesson examines various kinds of formal organizations, their impact upon American society and the kinds of leadership which are found in those organizations. It also notes the dissatisfaction which many individuals feel when so much of their lives is dominated by large organizations. We seem to recognize the need for complex formal organizations, whether in government, industry, or education. But we still do not like the depersonalization which comes with them. And we are skeptical of the leaders which political systems and television cameras develop for us. There appears to be a continuing historical hunger for the hero, the saint, the wise man to lead us to the promised land. Thus the paradox: a society dominated by bureaucracy in both its foundations and daily life yet filled with individuals who want and need to be accorded personal, individual treatment.

LEARNING OBJECTIVES

Knowledge Objectives

1 Define formal organization.

2 Describe a variety of formal organizations.

3 Define bureaucracy.

4 Describe Weber's analysis of bureaucracy.

5 Describe several dysfunctions of bureaucracy.

6 Describe the effect of formal organizations upon U.S. society.

Attitudinal Objective

Become more aware of the presence and dominance of large organizations in U.S. society and in your own life.

KEY TERMS

Formal organization   A group, usually large, created especially for a certain purpose, with rational guidelines.

Bureaucracy   An authority structure with hierarchy, specific written rules and procedures.

READING ASSIGNMENT

Robertson: *Sociology*, pp. 175–189

READING FOCUS QUESTIONS

1   What is a formal organization?

2   What are some different kinds of formal organizations?

3   What is a bureaucracy?

4   What are the typical features of bureaucracy according to Weber?

5   What are some dysfunctions of bureaucracy?

TV FOCUS QUESTIONS

1   How do sociologists use the term "formal organizations?"

2   Describe the continuum on which formal organizations may be located.

3   How did formal organizations come to be so dominant in U.S. society?

4   What are some dysfunctions of bureaucracies?

5   What is the future of formal organizations in U.S. society?

OPTIONAL ACTIVITY

Keep a log of every organization with which you interact for one week. Note which of these are of the voluntary type and which are of the profit-centered type.

POSTTEST

Multiple Choice

1 Formal organizations are characterized by all *except*
   a. rational design.
   b. specific objectives.
   c. impersonalization.
   d. informal relationships.

2 Which of these is on the voluntary end of the formal organization continuum?
   a. prison
   b. church
   c. factory
   d. police department

3 The key word for profit-centered formal organizations is
   a. values.
   b. progress.
   c. cohesion.
   d. efficiency.

4 The most significant characteristic of a bureaucracy is its
   a. efficiency.
   b. red tape.
   c. inefficiency.
   d. human concerns.

5 Max Weber's major concern about bureaucracy was its
   a. clear cut division of labor.
   b. hierarchy of authority.
   c. calculated subordination of human beings.
   d. written rules and procedures.

6 A major source of dysfunction in bureaucracies is their
   a. inability to handle unusual cases or situations.
   b. inefficiency in the average situation.
   c. office holders who lack expertise.
   d. adherence to rules and standard procedures.

7 The rise of formal organizations in U.S. society has affected
   a. the production of goods and services.
   b. voluntary organizations such as church and scouts.
   c. almost every aspect of daily life.
   d. all of these.

8 The future of formal organizations in U.S. society is likely to involve
   a. more dominance and depersonalization.
   b. more responsiveness to human values and needs.
   c. an increase in red tape.
   d. a decrease in their size.

POSTTEST ANSWERS

1 d (obj. 1, TV, Text, p. 175)
2 b (obj. 2, TV)
3 d (obj. 2, TV)
4 a (obj. 3, TV, Text, p. 176)
5 c (obj. 4, Text, p. 178)
6 a (obj. 5, Text, p. 181)
7 d (obj. 6, TV)
8 b (obj. 6, TV)

10

Deviance

SOCIOLOGICAL PERSPECTIVE

This lesson is about being different, really different, in a way that is negative and noticeable. When individuals are different in these terms, society discounts their identity and value. It often places a discount mark on them, similar to merchandise placed on sale because it is damaged or last year's style. When individuals are different in this manner, they are considered deviant. When their deviance is noticed by society and they have been marked, they are stigmatized. Being known as deviant poses problems in interaction for both the deviant and those interacting with the deviant.

A major characteristic of deviance is its relativity. Deviance is a matter of social definition, that is, a particular group or society defines a given act as deviant and it is so. Therefore, what is deviant varies from society to society and from time to time within a given society. This lesson looks at some examples of deviance and studies its characteristics. It also considers Emile Durkheim's classic suggestion that deviance is normal and functional in society.

LEARNING OBJECTIVES

Knowledge Objectives

   1 Define deviance.

   2 Identify the major theories of deviance.

   3 Describe the relative nature of deviance.

   4 Identify and describe some functions of deviance.

   5 Describe Durkheim's concept of deviance as normal.

   6 Recognize the widespread incidence of deviance in society.

Attitudinal Objectives

   1 Become more aware of the many ways in which people differ and become less judgmental of those who differ from us.

2 Value more fully the contributions made to society by some individuals who were at some time considered deviant.

KEY TERMS

Deviant One who differs negatively and noticeably from what is normal in society.

Relativity of deviance Variation in what is defined as deviant either within a society or among societies.

Functional deviance A situation in which breaking the rules is necessary or more practical than keeping them, as in cutting through red tape.

READING ASSIGNMENT

Robertson: *Sociology*, pp. 191–218

READING FOCUS QUESTIONS

1 What is deviance?

2 What are the major theories of deviance?

3 What are some major types of crime?

4 What are some functions of deviance?

TV FOCUS QUESTIONS

1 What is deviance?

2 What is meant by the relativity of deviance?

3 What are some examples of deviant behavior?

4 What are some functions of deviance?

5 Why is it not possible to eliminate deviance from a society?

OPTIONAL ACTIVITIES

1 Examine an anthropology text or reader, noticing the marriage, work, and religious customs of three or four different societies. How do these compare to U.S. society?

2 Talk with a few classmates or friends about what they consider to be acts of deviance. Do you agree with them?

3   Select two or three areas of behavior (for example, smoking, drinking alcoholic beverages, or driving autos) and create a continuum for behavior on each, from the worst to the best possible behavior. Locate yourself on that continuum five years ago and in the present.

POSTTEST

Multiple Choice

1   Deviant behavior is
   a. different and unusual.
   b. noticeable and admirable.
   c. negative and noticeable.
   d. negative and illegal.

2   Anomie theory holds that deviance has its major source in
   a. an imbalance in the social system.
   b. the flaws in individual character.
   c. an emphasis on affluence.
   d. an imbalance in the economic system.

3   The basis of the relativity of deviance is
   a. varied and changing value systems.
   b. a high degree of individualism.
   c. the presence or absence of rigid social control.
   d. the nature of the political system.

4   A major function of deviance is that it
   a. makes it easier to break the rules.
   b. helps to clarify the rules.
   c. causes the individual to feel less guilt.
   d. leads to greater ultimate conformity to rules.

5   Durkheim's concept of deviance as normal suggests that it is
   a. preferable to normal behavior.
   b. a sign of social illness and decay.
   c. a fundamental condition of society.
   d. inevitable that all individuals be deviant.

6   Deviance is widespread in society because
   a. people are natural rule-breakers.
   b. where there are rules, there must be deviance.
   c. individuals must be deviant to function.
   d. deviance is intrinsic to society.

POSTTEST ANSWERS

1 c (obj. 1, TV, Text, p. 191)
2 a (obj. 2, Text, p. 195)
3 a (obj. 3, TV)
4 b (obj. 4, TV)
5 c (obj. 5, TV)
6 d (obj. 6, TV)

11

Social Control

SOCIOLOGICAL PERSPECTIVE

Every society has rules which facilitate social order and stability. There is also a system of mechanisms to enforce the rules and to punish those who break them. This is called social control. It includes well known factors such as parents, schools, police, ministers, peer groups, and courts. It also includes such processes as internalization, the willing acceptance by an individual of the rule and its legitimacy. Most people obey most of the rules most of the time because they recognize the necessity of the rules.

When individuals break rules, they may be labeled as deviant. Many factors determine whether or not one is labeled deviant and how long the label sticks. This lesson examines those factors and several kinds of deviance. It also considers the ways in which deviant individuals cope with their problems. When an individual has been labeled as deviant, there are problems in interaction for both the deviant and those about the deviant. A major concept in the lesson is Goffman's idea of stigma, and of the master status created when one has been severely stigmatized.

Every individual carries about a social identity. The study of stigma is primarily an examination of the processes by which some identities become marked as less than whole and the effects of that mark upon both deviants and normals.

LEARNING OBJECTIVES

Knowledge Objectives

1 Define social control.

2 Describe different kinds of deviance.

3 Describe several stigma symbols.

4 Define labeling as a social process.

5 Define master status and describe its consequences.

6 Describe various coping mechanisms employed by deviant individuals.

Attitudinal Objectives

1 Become more aware of and appreciate more fully the role of various social control agencies in society.

2 Become more sensitive to and appreciate more fully the difficulties faced by people who are deviant.

3 Become more aware of one's own participation in the process of labeling others as deviant.

KEY TERMS

Social control   Ways and efforts of society to obtain compliance with its rules.

Stigma   The mark placed upon deviant individuals, whether physical or verbal.

Stigma symbol   Anything which represents or reveals an individual's deviance, such as skin color, a wheelchair, or prison stripes.

Labeling   The process by which society marks an individual as deviant.

Master status   A factor in one's social identity which dominates all other attributes and is the major point of identification.

Coping mechanism   A method, process, or item used by a deviant person to hide, reduce, or compensate for deviance.

READING ASSIGNMENT

Robertson: *Sociology*, pp. 191–218

READING FOCUS QUESTIONS

1 What is the labeling process?

2 How does one become labeled as a deviant?

3 What determines how well or poorly the label sticks?

4 What are some examples of labeling?

5 How do individuals attempt to cope with their labels?

TV FOCUS QUESTIONS

1 What is social control?

2 What are some ways in which social control is implemented?

3 What is labeling?

4 What are three major types of deviance?

5 What is stigma?

6 How does a person come to be labeled deviant?

7 What are some effects of labeling or stigma on interaction?

8 What are some ways employed by deviants to cope with stigma?

OPTIONAL ACTIVITIES

1 Talk with a person bearing a stigma label about the difficulties this creates and how those are managed.

2 Make a list of ten do's and ten don't's which you obey and then write beside each why you folllow them. What happened or would happen when you broke them?

POSTTEST

Multiple Choice

1 Social control
   a. guarantees high conformity to the rules.
   b. clarifies the rules well for everyone.
   c. encourages conformity and applies sanctions.
   d. seeks minimum conformity to the rules.

2 The type of deviance which includes racial stigma is
   a. tribal.
   b. character.
   c. body.
   d. moral.

3 Stigma symbols are
   a. always physical.
   b. both physical and verbal.
   c. always verbal.
   d. usually both physical and verbal.

4 Labeling is the process which
   a. causes the individual to become deviant.
   b. encourages the individual in deviance.
   c. prevents the individual from becoming deviant.
   d. identifies the individual as deviant.

5   A person is usually labeled as deviant after

   a. repeated acts of deviance.

   b. any act of deviance.

   c. any conviction of crime.

   d. many serious crimes.

6   In deviance theory, master status refers to the

   a. subordinate position of the deviant.

   b. advantage gained by deviance.

   c. central feature of social identity.

   d. advanced level of achievement.

7   One of the most common coping mechanisms employed by deviant individuals is

   a. insisting that others accept them as normal.

   b. claiming that deviance is not really bad.

   c. capitalizing on their deviance in social interaction.

   d. retreating to association with other deviants.

POSTTEST ANSWERS

1 c (obj. 1, Text, p. 193)

2 a (obj. 2, TV)

3 b (obj. 3, TV)

4 d (obj. 4, TV, Text, p. 198)

5 a (obj. 4, TV)

6 c (obj. 5, TV)

7 d (obj. 6, TV)

12

Social Inequality

SOCIOLOGICAL PERSPECTIVE

All of us are aware that there are people who have more or less money than we have, who live in larger or smaller houses than we live in, and who have more or less influence in the community than we have. This lesson is about the nature of all of this inequality and the sources from which it arises.

In all societies known to man, present and in history, there has been some degree of difference between the "have's" and the "have-not's." In some societies and times that difference has been very small. In most it is quite significant. This difference has a profound impact upon the life chances of individuals, that is, upon the likelihood that they will achieve a quality of life which includes physical well being, emotional satisfaction, longevity, and the goals which are important to them as individuals. Inequality is more than economic. It is social. It touches every aspect of life.

There is great variation from society to society in the nature and degree of social inequality. But a variable which is usually related closely to one's position in society is occupation. Occupation determines the amount of money and prestige one enjoys, or lacks. A troubling reality which we will discover in this lesson is that whatever society one examines, whatever social theory one uses to explain inequality, and whatever steps have been taken to reduce it, it persists as perhaps the most noticeable and important reality in any society.

LEARNING OBJECTIVES

Knowledge Objectives

1 Define social stratification.

2 Identify the criteria of class membership.

3 Define and contrast the functionalist and conflict theories of social stratification.

4 Discuss the nature of the gap between the "have's" and the "have-not's."

5 Explain why social inequality is universal and inevitable.

6 Identify the major source and location of power in the United States.

Attitudinal Objectives

1 Develop and greater understanding and appreciation of the nature and extent of social inequality in our own society.

2 Become more aware of the complexity and difficulty of trying to eliminate poverty and other forms of inequality.

KEY TERMS

Social inequality   A condition in which some individuals or groups have more or less than others in terms of money, influence, or power.

Social stratification   Structured inequality of large groups of people, usually called social classes, who have differential access to jobs, money, prestige, and power.

Life chances   The likelihood of obtaining the benefits of a society in terms of standard of living, personal goals, longevity.

Social mobility   Change from one status to another, for example, from working class to upper middle class.

READING ASSIGNMENT

Robertson: *Sociology*, pp. 251–266

READING FOCUS QUESTIONS

1 What is social inequality?

2 What is social mobility?

3 What are the criteria of class membership?

4 How do societies differ in the nature of their stratification systems?

5 What is the difference between functionalist and conflict ideology?

TV FOCUS QUESTIONS

1 How wide is the gap between myth and reality concerning equality in the United States?

2 What is social stratification?

3 What is the basis of stratification in the United States?

4 What is the evidence of a class system in the United States?

5 Where is the greatest power in the United States?

6 Why is stratification universal and inevitable?

OPTIONAL ACTIVITIES

1   Observe people around you throughout a day's activities and note material items about them which indicate status, such as clothing, cars, equipment, jewelry, furniture. Separate the people you have observed into low, middle, and high status categories. Note the occupations of each category.

2   Ask five people of low status and five of high status why people have different status. Compare the answers.

POSTTEST

Multiple Choice

1   Social stratification is
    a. differences in taste in food and clothing.
    b. based upon racial differences.
    c. differences in religion and politics.
    d. structured inequality of large categories of people.

2   Social class membership is
    a. mostly a matter of individual judgment.
    b. based upon one important variable.
    c. based upon a complex combination of variables.
    d. very difficult to determine.

3   The conflict theory of inequality emphasizes
    a. solidarity and harmony.
    b. exploitation and injustice.
    c. the value of the *status quo*.
    d. the value of slow change.

4   The gap between the "have's" and the "have-nots"
    a. remains very large, in spite of the American myth of equality.
    b. is largely a matter of how people see differences in occupational prestige.
    c. has been greatly reduced by the massification process.
    d. is being reduced by new ideas in economics and politics.

5   Social inequality is universal and inevitable because
    a. political systems differ from society to society.
    b. society accords higher reward to some labor than to other labor.
    c. no attempts have been made to reform economic and political injustice.
    d. some people don't want good life chances.

6 The major power in the United States is found in
   a. military complexes.
   b. nationally famous universities.
   c. corporate headquarters.
   d. the White House.

POSTTEST ANSWERS

1 d (obj. 1, TV, Text, p. 253)
2 c (obj. 2, TV, Text, p. 255)
3 b (obj. 3, Text, p. 265)
4 a (obj. 4, TV)
5 b (obj. 5, TV)
6 c (obj. 6, TV)

13

U.S. Social Classes

SOCIOLOGICAL PERSPECTIVE

Drive down a crowded freeway and note the types of cars people drive, from Cadillacs to clunkers. Attend a pro ball game and note the end zone seats and the private boxes, and the seat you are in. Walk across a downtown pedestrian mall and observe the clothing and passersby, from three-piece-suits and fancy skirts to polyester slacks and blue denim. Compare the prices of cars in various church parking lots on Sunday morning. Look around at people and the material objects which they use—whether you are at work, at play, on vacation, in court, or at church—and you will observe differences.

Beyond these differences in outward appearances are more subtle and important differences in beliefs, values, and behavior patterns. The rich are different from the poor in ways beyond the amount of money and possessions each has. This lesson is a study of those differences by using a concept which social scientists have created under the term social class. This concept and others associated with it enable us to organize and focus the realities which exist in society in terms of differences or inequalities in wealth, status, and power.

Probably no other factor has such tremendous influence upon one's life chances as does the social class into which one is born. Class is a powerful influence upon attitudes, values, beliefs, and behavior patterns. It affects work, education, religion, family, recreation, politics, and most other dimensions of daily life. There are many variations among individuals within any social class. The picture is very complex and the danger of oversimplification and stereotyping is quite real. But a careful look at some of the basics of the American social class system offers valuable insights into attitudes and behavior.

We will observe five social classes and the types of work and kinds of concerns typical of each class.

LEARNING OBJECTIVES

Knowledge Objectives

1 Define social class.

2 Identify five social classes in American society.

3   Describe the occupational and values profile of each class.

4   Describe some effects of class membership upon behavior.

5   Describe the continuing significance of social class in American society.

Attitudinal Objectives

1   Become more aware of the existence and significance of social class in our society.

2   Appreciate more fully the impact upon your own life of your social class status.

KEY TERMS

Social class   A very large number of individuals who occupy a similar position relative to the market place and hold similar values and beliefs.

Status inconsistency   A condition evident when one's income is high but is derived from a low prestige job—or when any two determinants of social class position are out of synch.

Social mobility   Movement from one social class to another, whether upward or downward, or movement within a social class.

Massification   The process in which the visibility of social class lines is blurred by mass population, mass consumption, anonymity, informality of dress and life style.

READING ASSIGNMENT

Robertson: *Sociology*, pp. 266–276

READING FOCUS QUESTIONS

1   What is the basis of the American class system?

2   How much difference is there between the top fifth and the bottom fifth of American population?

3   What are the five social classes in the United States?

4   What are some correlates of class membership?

TV FOCUS QUESTIONS

1   What is a social class?

2   What are the major determinants of social class position?

3   What is the massification process?

4 What are the five social classes in the United States and what are their major characteristics?

5 What indicates the continuing importance of class in U.S. society?

OPTIONAL ACTIVITIES

1 Determine your own social class position by consulting data and charts in the text. Compare what the lesson says individuals in your class believe and do with what you know of reality in your own life.

2 Ask five people of various occupational rank to list American social classes and give an example of an occupation in each. Compare the answers with those in the lesson.

3 Sit in a shopping mall and observe individuals' actions, clothing, and habits and see if you can determine their social class position.

POSTTEST

True–False

1 A social class is any very large number of people who enjoy the same kind of sports and entertainment.

2 Social class membership involves not only the amount of money one has or makes, but also the source of that money and the use of it.

3 The major difference between the upper class and the upper middle class is the amount of money each has.

4 A major characteristic of those in the very top of the upper class is the sense of family, tradition, and grace associated with great wealth.

5 Many people in the upper middle class think of themselves as having careers or positions, not jobs.

6 Upper middle class people have the most stable marriages and lower middle class people attend church more.

7 The key word for the lower middle class is "respectability" because they "have it made."

8 Because members of the working class are not on the success ladder and have low expectations of life, there is very little which they enjoy.

9 The working class attitude toward the lower class is one of sympathy and understanding, based primarily upon the relative closeness of the two classes in neighborhoods and on jobs.

10 Major economic, political, and social advances in the past two decades have made social class position less important.

POSTTEST ANSWERS

1 F (obj. 1, TV)
2 T (obj. 1, TV)
3 F (obj. 2, TV, Text, p. 271)
4 T (obj. 3, TV, Text, p. 271)
5 T (obj. 3, TV)
6 T (obj. 4, TV)
7 F (obj. 3, 4, TV)
8 F (obj. 4, TV)
9 F (obj. 3, 4, TV)
10 F (obj. 5, TV)

14

Poverty

SOCIOLOGICAL PERSPECTIVE

How long has it been since you drove through a poor area? Most Americans have become unfamiliar with poverty. Not only do nine out of ten not live in poverty, but most of those nine no longer come very close to it in their daily rounds. The only people who see the poor are the poor and the professionals who deal with them: social workers, policemen, health clinics, courts, meter men, and church workers.

A few decades ago, poverty was just across the tracks. Cities were smaller. Highways passed through small towns and through cities at ground level. The traveler, whether going to work or across country, drove through the areas of a city which were poor or through the shack towns and sharecropper areas of rural and small town life. The poor looked poor. And we were all moving slowly enough to recognize them when we saw them. Today the freeways bypass the ghettos; we now move through them so rapidly we no longer see the poverty. The interstates bypass the small towns, and rural poverty is seen only at a distance, if at all. The suburban shopping centers keep most suburbanites out of the central city and the declining areas.

America is crowded, busy, pleasure-oriented, successful. There is work, football, television, the movies, disco, Vegas, and church. But there is an underside to American society. There are those who do not participate in the familiar world of work, progress, aspiration, success, and personal happiness. Their resources are too meager. Their strategy is for daily survival. Even in America, that strategy sometimes fails.

Strategies for survival come in all forms and make little sense to most of us. A mother on the seventh floor of an apartment building was criticized for "air mailing" her garbage. She merely threw the bags of garbage out of her window to the alley below. This seems such an unneighborly, anti-community minded act. What kind of person must she be? She is a mother of three small children who must be left alone in an apartment endangered by rats if she is to make the seven flight walk down to the alley with the garbage and then back up stairways frequented by drug addicts and others who give her legitimate cause to fear for her safety. Given these circumstances, she made a simple, logical decision and threw her garbage out the window. Not only have very few Americans ever thrown their garbage out the window, but more importantly, few have experienced the conditons which make that behavior appropriate. The point is that not many Americans understand poverty or the behavior of those who are poor. This lesson is a look at life on the bottom, what it is like, who is there, and what is going to happen to it.

There is a new poverty which arises from the post-industrial revolution, or what is perhaps better named the "information society." The great masses of American workers were employed, until recently, in major production industries such as autos, steel, rubber, and textiles. The development of technology in these areas, along with worldwide competition in labor, has forced American industry to turn to hi-tech computers and robots and foreign human labor to produce items for the competitive marketplace. When robots or foreign labor will do the job for $5 an hour, industry cannot pay American workers $15 an hour for that work. The foreign labor rate will not support U.S. workers in traditional fashion, so they decline the job.

This change has displaced millions of workers from traditional sources of employment in the U.S. economy, forcing them to retire early, scratch for some incidental job, go on welfare, or retrain for the higher-technology economy. Many of the displaced jobs required skills learned in a few days or hours. The new technology typically requires months or years of education or training at the expense of government, private industry, or the individual. This must be done at a time of low morale for the displaced worker. Additionally, in many cases, these retraining workers must do exactly what they did not want to do when they quit school early to take working-class jobs: sit at desks in classrooms and read material that is now more difficult than the reading they disliked a decade earlier.

There is little doubt that many displaced workers will find their way eventually into the new economy and have jobs that pay as well or better than before. But these are complex times and the process of change and retraining is complex. There may be an increase in poverty from this source and its character will be different. These people have worked for generations. They have pride, aspirations, organizational skills, and guns. If things should really go badly for them, they will bring a new dimension to poverty.

LEARNING OBJECTIVES

Knowledge Objectives

1 Define poverty in absolute and relative terms.

2 Identify the causes of poverty.

3 Identify various attitudes toward poverty.

4 Identify the extent of poverty in the United States.

5 Describe life conditions of the poor.

6 Discuss the nature of the gap between the "have's" and the "have-not's" in the United States.

Attitudinal Objectives

1 Become more aware of the nature and extent of poverty in our society.

2 Develop a greater sensitivity to the problems of the poor.

KEY TERMS

Absolute deprivation   A condition in which individuals lack the basic necessities of life.

Relative deprivation   A condition in which individuals lack the resources to maintain a near average standard of living.

Culture of poverty   A concept which holds that for many poor individuals poverty is a distinctive way of life with its own set of values, beliefs, and behavior patterns.

Poverty level   An income level determined by the federal government, usually stated in terms of the money needed for a non-farm family of four to purchase the basic necessities of life.

READING ASSIGNMENT

Robertson: *Sociology*, pp. 276–281

READING FOCUS QUESTIONS

1   What is the difference between absolute and relative deprivation?

2   How many poor are in the United States?

3   What are the major causes of poverty?

4   What are the prevailing social attitudes toward poverty?

TV FOCUS QUESTIONS

1   Why do most Americans not see much of poverty today?

2   What is absolute deprivation? How does it differ from relative deprivation?

3   How many Americans live in poverty?

4   What is the nature and the impact of the gap between the poor and the non-poor?

5   How has the position of the poor relative to the non-poor relative changed in the past few decades?

6   Who are the "hard core" poor and why are they thus labeled?

OPTIONAL ACTIVITIES

1   Drive through the most poor area in your city or suburb noting conditions of houses, streets, yards, and playgrounds. Then drive through the most expensive housing area and note the same items.

2 Pretend that you are 22, married, have two children, dropped out of high school, have no special job skills. Develop a family budget. Check the classifieds for a job which pays enough to meet that budget—and for which you qualify.

POSTTEST
Multiple Choice

1 Absolute deprivation is the
   a. certainty that people are poor.
   b. lack of basic necessities.
   c. lack of will to work.
   d. only meaningful way to define poverty.

2 Relative deprivation is a definition of poverty which
   a. compares the income of the lowest portion of society with the rest of society.
   b. ignores those in absolute poverty.
   c. compares the poor only to rich people.
   d. excludes the poor who can provide themselves with basic necessities.

3 The concept known as "the culture of poverty" holds that
   a. the poor enjoy their life.
   b. there is no solution to poverty.
   c. the poor have internalized a sense of fatalism and despair.
   d. the behavior of the poor is an irrational response to reality.

5 American attitudes toward poverty include the idea that
   a. the poor are poor because they prefer not to work.
   b. airlines and railroads are subsidized so why not the poor?
   c. most people on welfare are old, very young, or unable to work.
   d. giving poor people a little welfare will encourage them to supplement that with work.

6 Using the absolute deprivation definition of poverty, the number of poor in the United States is about one in
   a. 4.
   b. 10.
   c. 30.
   d. 50.

7 Living conditions of the poor in the United States
   a. have not improved in absolute terms in the past 30 years.
   b. have little effect upon the aspiration of the poor.
   c. are well known and understood by most Americans.
   d. are better in absolute terms but unchanged in relation to the rest of society.

8 The share of the national income of the bottom fifth of American families
   a. was about 5% in 1940 and 1980.
   b. was about 5% in 1940 and 10% in 1980.
   c. is gradually increasing.
   d. is gradually declining.

9 The "hard core" poor are so labeled because
   a. they are so determined to remain poor.
   b. their actual conditions are worse than any other poor.
   c. their condition has been unchanged by all of the social and economic events of the past few decades.
   d. they are the most highly motivated of the poor.

POSTTEST ANSWERS

1 b (obj. 1, TV, Text, p. 277)
2 a (obj. 1, TV, Text, p. 276)
3 c (obj. 2, TV)
4 a (obj. 3, Text, p. 278)
5 b (obj. 4, TV)
6 d (obj. 5, TV)
7 a (obj. 6, TV)
8 c (obj. 6, TV)

15

Minorities

SOCIOLOGICAL PERSPECTIVE

Is the United States really a melting pot society in which people of all races, colors, and creeds participate equally in the grand democratic experience of freedom, progress, and success? How do you feel about people who differ from you in these respects? What influences your behavior toward those who are different? What is the present status of minority groups in America?

These are complex and difficult questions. In this lesson, you will examine the definitions of race, ethnicity, minority group, prejudice, discrimination. This should help you come to understand more fully the actual condition of various groups in society as well as the sources of your feelings about yourself and those groups.

It is not sufficient to define race and ethnicity in biological terms. First, there is no adequate definition in this regard. Second, the far more important factor is the social definition of these terms. What is important is the meaning which people attach to physical differences and how that influences their treatment of groups with those differences.

This lesson emphasizes the social origins of racism, the experiences of minority groups in the United States, and the present status of such groups.

In the history of civil rights groups and movements since 1950, one must observe that the peace and prosperity of the 1950's contributed greatly to the success of civil rights movements in the 1960's. It was the right time for a few dreamers, liberal politicians, and church leaders to call moderate Americans to a new level of social justice for minorities. The Big War was behind us. Jobs were good. Everyone was going to school and building new houses. Color had come to TV and Interstate 55 was really smooth. Why not do the right thing and give them a break?

By the late 1970's, things had changed dramatically. Interest rates were very high. Inflation was just as high. Energy troubles were merely highlighted by the long gas lines. The nation had seen the rise of several new minorities, each claiming a share of the nation's attention, justice, and resources. Traditional minority concerns were merely pushed off center stage, off TV and the front page, and out of the consciousness of most Americans.

By the mid-1980's, new voices began to be heard, especially from America's most visible minority group, the blacks. Those voices speak of a new strategy for growing problems in the ghetto. The old strategy of civil rights, welfare, and government programs is viewed as perpetuating poverty and dependence. There is a call for revision of welfare and emphasis on individual responsibility for behavior, especially in the area of marriage and family life.

In a time of growing problems in the world community and increased disorganization in the ghetto, both those in the culture of poverty and those in roles of power and decision making seem to face some difficult and critical choices.

LEARNING OBJECTIVES

Knowledge Objectives

1 Define such terms as race, ethnicity, and minority group.

2 Make a distinction between prejudice and discrimination and illustrate each.

3 Identify the major minority groups in the United States.

4 Describe the historical experience of blacks in the United States.

5 Explain the relationship between the rise of new minority groups and the loss of focus upon minority groups in general.

6 Explain the relationship between present national concerns and the decline of interest in minority needs.

7 Identify various attitudes toward the concept of the melting pot.

Attitudinal Objectives

1 Develop an understanding and appreciation of the sources of prejudice and discrimination in society and of the struggle of minority groups to improve their life chances.

2 Be more aware of the pluralistic makeup of our society and of the strains which that places upon many individuals.

3 Understand and appreciate more fully the changes over time of the attitude of majority groups toward minority groups.

KEY TERMS

Race   A social definition placed upon a large number of people who are perceived to have certain visible physical characteristics.

Ethnic group   A large number of people who because of certain shared cultural traits and high mutual interaction regard themselves and are thought of by others as being a distinctive group.

Minority group   A large group of individuals who because of perceived physical or social differences are defined as being different and are accorded unequal treatment.

Prejudice   A negative attitude toward individuals or groups which is based upon assumptions or stereotypes.

Discrimination   The behavior by individuals or groups toward members of any group which limits that group's access to rights, opportunities, or resources and is based upon prejudice.

Institutionalized discrimination   The unequal treatment of members of groups which is built-in to the institutions and customs of a society.

READING ASSIGNMENT

Robertson: *Sociology*, pp. 283–311

READING FOCUS QUESTIONS

1   Define race, ethnicity, minority group.

2   Distinguish between prejudice and discrimination.

3   Identify the major minority groups in the United States.

TV FOCUS QUESTIONS

1   What is the basis upon which majority groups discriminate against minority groups?

2   What is the history of blacks in the United States?

3   How does the average American feel about minorities today?

4   What has been the effect upon minority groups of the rise of several new minorities?

5   What are the major national issues which have contributed to a loss of focus upon minority needs in the 1970's and 1980's?

6   How do various interpretations of the melting pot concept relate to minority issues today?

OPTIONAL ACTIVITIES

1   Discuss with members of a minority group (other than your own) the experiences they have had in childhood, school, dating, employment, and other life areas, and compare them with your own.

2   Conduct a mini-poll of ten individuals among your classmates or friends or family on attitudes toward minority group needs in the present.

POSTTEST

Multiple Choice

1 The major element in a functional definition of race is
   a. physical characteristics.
   b. cultural traits.
   c. social definition of characteristics or traits.
   d. all of these.

2 A major problem in racial classification is that
   a. there are no major differences among people.
   b. all of the differences are too subjective to evaluate.
   c. there are many individuals who cannot be fitted neatly into such classifications.

3 Which of the following is *not* true of minority groups?
   a. The members suffer disadvantages from other groups.
   b. Groups are identified by characteristics which are socially visible.
   c. Most minority groups members are born into such groups.
   d. Groups rarely identify themselves as distinctive from the majority population.

4 Prejudice differs from discrimination in that one
   a. involves attitudes and the other involves behavior.
   b. is directed at individuals and the other at groups.
   c. is based upon biology and the other upon experience.
   d. all of these.

5 Major minority groups in the United States include all *except*
   a. Blacks.
   b. Native Americans.
   c. Hispanics.
   d. WASP's.

6 Stages through which blacks have passed in the United States include all *except*
   a. chattle slavery.
   b. economic exploitation and discrimination.
   c. equal civil rights on the law books.
   d. equal opportunity and affirmative action.
   e. equality of income and job opportunity.

7 The rise of new minority groups has affected the total minority picture in that
   a. traditional minority groups must now face additional competition for limited national resources.

b. most people no longer consider the traditional minority groups as true minorities.

c. there are now so many minority groups demanding help that many Americans merely turn a deaf ear.

d. a and c.

e. all of these.

8 Pressing national concerns such as energy, inflation, and crime have affected minority movements in that

a. most Americans have put minority needs "on the back burner" while facing their own problems.

b. these concerns have caused many Americans to feel that they are victims and unable to help others.

c. the competition for jobs and other resources has made Americans less sympathetic to minority needs.

d. all of these.

9 Minority attitudes toward the melting pot concept tend to differ from majority attitudes in that

a. one wishes to join American society and maintain minority cultural values while the other expects to share completely in mainstream cultural values.

b. one emphasizes domestic concerns and the other foreign.

c. one places emphasis on race and the other on economics.

10 The melting pot concept has

a. meant different things to different people in the United States.

b. elements of myth in that immigrants, minorities, and ethnic groups have never really lost their identities.

c. in reality functioned to create a society of pluralism.

d. all of these.

POSTTEST ANSWERS

1 c (obj. 1, TV, Text, p. 284)
2 c (obj. 1, Text, p. 286)
3 d (obj. 1, Text, p. 287)
4 a (obj. 2, Text, p. 293)
5 d (obj. 3, TV)
6 e (obj. 4, TV)
7 d (obj. 5, TV)
8 d (obj. 6, TV)
9 a (obj. 7, TV)
10 d (obj. 7, TV)

Social Institutions

16

The Family

SOCIOLOGICAL PERSPECTIVE

You are born into a family and there you receive the care necessary to sustain life, to grow to maturity, and to take your place in the adult work of the next generation. Almost everyone in early to middle adulthood marries and participates in the on-going cycle of human society.

The family is familiar to almost everyone. Its influence and its concerns are prominent in the daily lives of most people. It makes a major contribution toward meeting the most basic needs of human beings. What the family does for us is so ordinary that it is often taken for granted. In this lesson, we will examine the functions of the family which exist in almost all cultures. We will call these "family universals." By examining these functions, we will not only see more clearly what the family actually does, but we will also understand more fully why the family has endured through time and why it is highly likely to endure in the future.

One of the most interesting realities about family life is that it differs from society to society. It is easy to see that families in an agricultural society earn their living differently from families in an industrial society. It is less obvious but equally important for us to observe that those same families manage differently such matters as family money, authority, child care, and conflict.

This lesson on the family should make you more aware of the historical, universal role of the family in human society, and of the many ways in which families differ. It should also cause you to think of the ways in which your own family has influenced your life, contributed to your well being, and given you a push toward the future. As you read the text and watch the program, look closely. Somewhere in the process you will likely see yourself and your family.

LEARNING OBJECTIVES

Knowledge Objectives

1 Define family.

2 Describe the functions of the family in most cultures.

3 Describe cross-cultural variations in ways in which families perform their functions.

4 Explain why the family endures in spite of great change.

5 Explain the change in the economic function of the family in industrial societies.

6 Identify several characteristics of the contemporary American family.

7 Explain why the nuclear family functions well in industrial societies.

Attitudinal Objectives

1 Develop a better understanding and appreciation of the role of the family in human society.

2 Develop a greater knowledge and respect for differences in the family from one society to another.

3 Recognize and appreciate more fully the place of one's own family in the beginning and continuation of life.

KEY TERMS

Family A relatively permanent group of people related by marriage who live together as an economic unit and whose adults share sexual relationships and assume responsibility for their children.

Marriage An official contract approving a sexual union of relative permanence between one or more males and one or more females.

Polygamy A marital practice in which either a male or female is married to two or more persons of the opposite sex at the same time.

Extended family Two or more generations of the same kinship lineage which live in close proximity.

Nuclear family A husband and wife and their dependent children.

Family universals Functions which are performed by families in all societies.

Cross-cultural variations Ways in which societies differ in beliefs or behavior patterns.

READING ASSIGNMENT

Robertson: *Sociology*, pp. 347–357

READING FOCUS QUESTIONS

1 What is the definition of "family"?

2 How has the economic function of the family changed from pre-industrial to industrial society?

3 Name four major characteristics of the contemporary American family.

4 Why is the nuclear family more functional than the extended family in industrial society?

TV FOCUS QUESTIONS

1 What are the four major functions of the family in most cultures?

2 Select two functions of the family and discuss variations among cultures in fulfilling these functions.

3 Why does the institution of family survive and remain vital in spite of great social changes?

OPTIONAL ACTIVITIES

1 Determine the structure of your grandparents' families and compare it to the structure of your own family in terms of size, authority, division of labor and attitudes toward children, sex, and work.

2 Ask several people over 65 why they married. Ask several people under 30 why they married. Compare the answers and look for changes in family functions.

POSTTEST

Multiple Choice

1 A family is defined as
   a. a group of individuals living in the same house.
   b. two people who share sexual activities regularly.
   c. married individuals living together, sharing sex, child care and economics.
   d. two or more blood relatives sharing a residence.

2 Functions of the family in most cultures include all *except*
   a. regulation of sex.
   b. socialization of children.
   c. limiting the number of marital partners.
   d. economic cooperation.

3 Cross-cultural variations found in the family include the
   a. number of adults in the marriage.
   b. location of power in the family.
   c. existence of an incest taboo.
   d. a and b.

4 The family remains vital and important through time because
   a. there are no alternative life styles.
   b. it is the best known way to produce humans who function well in society.
   c. cultural values prohibit any alternative.
   d. tradition favors the family so strongly.

5 The only universal norm for family life in all cultures is
   a. people must eventually marry.
   b. the incest taboo that prohibits sexual intercourse between certain relatives.
   c. people may not mate with anyone they choose.
   d. b and c.

6 The pattern of authority which prevails in the family in most societies is
   a. patriarchal.
   b. matriarcal.
   c. egalitarian.
   d. a and c.

7 The major change in the economic function of the family as a society develops from agrarian to industrial is
   a. greater production of goods by the family unit.
   b. a change in work rules for the family members.
   c. less production and greater consumption of goods by the family unit.

8 The contemporary American family is characterized by all *except*
   a. monogamous.
   b. nuclear.
   c. egalitarian.
   d. extended.

9 In agricultural societies, the extended family functions well because it
   a. is a self-contained work unit which meets labor needs.
   b. encourages individual success and mobility.
   c. controls sexual activities.
   d. a and b.

10 The small, detached nuclear family functions well in an industrial society because
   a. the authority structure of the family is better.
   b. children are more highly motivated to contribute to the family.
   c. it is a mobile, flexible, independent unit.
   d. a and c.

POSTTEST ANSWERS

1 c   (obj. 1, Text, p. 348)
2 c   (obj. 2, TV, Text, p. 349)
3 d   (obj. 3, TV, Text, p. 352)
4 b   (obj. 4, TV)
5 d   (obj. 3, Text, p. 352)
6 a   (obj. 3, Text, p. 354)
7 c   (obj. 5, Text, p. 355)
8 d   (obj. 6, Text, p. 358)
9 a   (obj. 5, Text, p. 355)
10 c   (obj. 7, Text, p. 357)

17

The Changing American Family

SOCIOLOGICAL PERSPECTIVE

Why do people marry? Ask a village leader among the Melpa of New Guinea and he will say, "To have someone to take care of the pigs and garden." Ask a woman in that same village and she will say, "To have a garden, a hut, and some pigs to care for." When various cultures through time have been examined—including U.S. culture in all but its most recent years—we discover that an economic variable emerges as very significant and primary in people's reasons for marriage. Although economics is still an important element in American marriage, our question asked of Americans today is likely to receive a quite different answer, probably something such as, "To be happy," or "Because I love someone." When one has examined all the evidence, read all the polls, and looked carefully at contemporary American marriage and family life, the essence of the matter seems to be that Americans marry to find personal happiness. This essence must be kept in mind as we examine the current status of American marriage and family. It is not only why people marry. It is also why they have fewer children, save less money, divorce more readily and frequently, engage in more extra-marital affairs, change jobs more readily, and give less money to church. American culture is pervaded by the individual happiness syndrome; its impact upon marriage and family is profound.

We remember that "culture" is essentially how people live, the total of their values, beliefs, and behavior patterns. In a comparative sense, the United States has never been a traditional culture as have many which see very little change through decades or even centuries. But the United States of pre-World War II was clearly different from the United States of today in many significant ways. It was more rural, less educated, more religious, more homogeneous. It moved at a slower pace. It knew its neighbors. Relationships were more permanent. The dominant values were family, work, church, country. Generally, confidence in social institutions such as marriage, religion, government, was high. Individuals believed that the path to happiness and success lay in conformity to the expectations and rules which were legitimated by these institutions. The family was more important than the individual. People expected to stay married—and did, for the sake of the kids, the church, the family. Many of these did not expect to be happy. Like Charlie Brown, they were content not to be unhappy.

The family has, historically, in all cultures been functional in work, economics, religion, and education—as well as child-rearing and companionship. The decline of family involvement and influence in all but the last area has great significance for the stability of the family. Marriage has become more firmly—and for some almost exclusively—tied to personal emotional satisfaction and happiness, rather than to practical needs relating to work, housing, social approval. As we proceed through the lesson, we will find this to be the most important reality touching marriage and family life in the United States today.

In the mid-1980's the divorce rate showed a slight decline for the first time in three decades. Many complex variables are involved in this picture, such as age at first marriage, the option of living together without marriage, the condition of the economy, and the apparent ending of the sexual revolution of the 1960's and 1970's. In spite of a continued high divorce rate, the marriage rate remains high and most divorced people eventually remarry.

One can make a good speculative case for the anticipation of a continuing flat divorce rate by observing that many of the factors that figured into the rise of the rate have about run their course. Most women are working, the birth rate is about as low as it will go, the decline of religion seems to have bottomed out, and the option of living together without marriage has been somewhat normalized. Generally, women are getting a better deal in marriage and men are gradually adjusting to all of these changes.

A major variable that rises as a specter over our optimism is the cumulative effect of a long-term high divorce rate. The United States has seen more than one million divorces a year for over ten years, involving more than a million children each year. Research is only now beginning to make clear the long-term consequences for individuals who have experienced parental divorce at various ages. Those divorcing in the 1970's and 1980's did so out of a parental and societal background of a low divorce rate with social support systems rather well intact. Those divorcing in the 1990's and beyond may be doing so in a social system of greater fragility.

LEARNING OBJECTIVES

Knowledge Objectives

1. Describe the current status of the American family.
2. Identify various factors affecting mate selection in the United States.
3. Discuss the major reasons why people in the United States marry.
4. Identify the major changes in reasons for marriage in the past few decades of American life.
5. Identify social variables which relate to a high divorce rate.
6. Discuss the effect of the changing role of women upon divorce rates.
7. Discuss the special vulnerability of the nuclear family.
8. Identify trends which social scientists expect to continue into the next few decades.

Attitudinal Objectives

1   Develop a greater awareness and appreciation of the degree of fragility associated with today's American marriages and the reasons for that fragility.

2   Develop a greater sensitivity to one's own marital expectations and the extent to which these are realistic and feasible.

KEY TERMS

Nuclear family   A husband and wife and their dependent children.

Socialization of children   All of the influences which contribute to learning and practicing cultural values and beliefs, a process which begins in the family and is a continuing major function of the family.

Social change   Variations in the nature of human relationships, rules, institutions, and practices.

Divorce rate   The number of divorces per 1,000 population in a given year.

READING ASSIGNMENT

Robertson: *Sociology,* pp. 357–373

READING FOCUS QUESTIONS

1   What is typical about the American family?

2   What are the basic functions of romantic love?

3   What are some social factors affecting mate selection?

4   What are the major causes of divorce?

5   What are some trends in the future of marriage and family?

TV FOCUS QUESTIONS

1   How have individuals' reasons for marrying changed in the United States?

2   How does the individual's need for happiness relate to marriage and to a high divorce rate?

3   How have expectations in marriage changed?

4   What are the most significant changes in marital roles?

5   Why is the nuclear family vulnerable to divorce?

6   What trends seem likely to continue in the future of marriage?

OPTIONAL ACTIVITIES

1   Select two or three married couples who both work and ask each person why the woman works and how it affects the marriage. Compare male and female answers.

2 Do some library, newspaper, or journal research on reasons people give for divorce. Make a list of the reasons and determine how many of them relate to the search for personal happiness.

POSTTEST

True–False

1 Currently, the typical American family is monogamous, endogamous, and nuclear.

2 The American family has been historically patriarchal and, in spite of changes in women's roles, there has been little change in the authority structure of the family.

3 Most people in the United States marry individuals who are similar to themselves in age, social class, religion, education, and physical characteristics.

4 In spite of television's portrayal of romantic love, most Americans marry for rational, practical reasons.

5 A major change in reasons for marriage is the reduction of the importance of economics and the increase in the search for personal happiness.

6 Social variables which relate to the high divorce rate include the changing roles of women, sexual permissiveness, and eased divorce laws.

7 American culture contradicts itself in that it values individual freedom and happiness at a time in which the family is needed to meet people's needs for intimacy, security, and belonging.

8 The growing independence of women, achieved primarily through work roles, generally strengthens the nuclear family and stabilizes marriages.

9 Although the roles of women in marriage have changed greatly in the past two decades, it seems to have had little effect upon men.

10 Although the nuclear family today has less assistance from relatives in child care and economic matters, the very strong mutual dependency of husband and wife stabilizes the family, especially after the children have left home.

11 Present indications are that the high divorce rate, alternative lifestyles, and a continued emphasis upon personal fulfillment will decrease the importance of marriage and family in the near future.

POSTTEST ANSWERS

1 T (obj. 1, Text, p. 358)
2 F (obj. 1, Text, p. 358)
3 T (obj. 2, Text, p. 360)
4 F (obj. 3, TV)
5 T (obj. 4, TV, Text, p. 362)
6 T (obj. 5, TV, Text, p. 362)

7 T (obj. 5, TV)
8 F (obj. 6, TV)
9 F (obj. 6, TV)
10 F (obj. 7, TV)
11 F (obj. 8, TV)

18

Education

SOCIOLOGICAL PERSPECTIVE

Every society has a way to transmit to its young the skills and information required for them to participate as functioning members of that society. In simple societies, this process is informal, involving mostly the daily activities of family and community. Children and young people learn to do what they need to learn by actually doing it. In all advanced, industrial societies, the process is formal and systematized and is called education.

In the United States, expectations of education are very high. In recent decades they have become even higher. National and community political and opinion leaders decided that the schools should educate not only in the basic skills required for literacy and job performance but also in such areas as race relations, driving safety, drug abuse, sex and family life, and actual on-the-job training. The extent and complexity of these expectations undoubtedly contribute to both the problems and disappointments found in education today.

Many social problems exist in America: racism, family disintegration, violence, poverty, drug abuse. The problems are in the nature of the total society—its political, economic, social structure. The schools do not create poverty. They have many poor children to teach. They do not create illiteracy. They are committed to eradicating it. The schools did not segregate neighborhoods. They are reflections of the values and conditions of people in the neighborhoods. These social problems are not caused by the schools, but they come to school on the bus and in the cars. The schools are in the center of efforts to deal with these problems.

Much education today is attempted under physical and psychological conditions which make success impossible. Heavily crowded urban schools, inadequate staff and facilities, and very serious discipline problems make many schools either a blackboard jungle or a joke. Many of the nation's high school teachers work in constant fear of physical assault. Some carry handguns. Policemen patrol school hallways.

Beyond these realities are the general cultural values which are highlighted in advertising, on television, and in the behavior of many adults. A leisure-oriented, pleasure-seeking adult society which copes with its own problems by turning to drugs, sex, violence, and alcohol can hardly be surprised when individuals in high school and college try the same escape mechanisms. These behavioral patterns create a social environment, a psychological climate, which distracts youth from reality, hard work, and the development of their minds and skills through the traditional educational process. There is lowered creativity, self-discipline, and future orientation in such an atmosphere. A society which seems preoccupied with finding someone to "help me make it through the night" still expects schools to prepare young people to face life with knowledge, skills, and functional attitudes.

A growing problem area is the increasing number and proportion of students in high school who work during the school year. A teacher recognizes working students by noting those who are asleep in her eight o'clock class. They tell her it's the only time they have to sleep. Family structure of the 1980's, U.S. culture which sells instant fun through material possessions, and a powerful peer group combine to cause American young people to sacrifice their educational and occupational future for a car and stereo today.

The schools do contribute to their own problems. They are highly bureaucratized with the accompanying administrative overkill. Poor teachers continue to teach. Paperwork and educational doublespeak hinder good teachers. The system has its own ills, ambiguities, defense mechanisms, and vested interests.

The essence of this lesson is that education gets blamed for a lot of failure that started somewhere else. As an institution, its life and problems are intricately related to many other social institutions.

Somewhere between freshman orientation in the fall and senior commencement in the spring, there are searching questions to be asked about the functions of education in America and the relationship between education and our total society.

The late 1980's are a time of growing concern about the quality of education. Signs of the times are tests for teachers and tests for high school diplomas. The key words are responsibility, accountability, and performance. What is ultimately troubling in this scene is that the tests, the standards, and the achievements are all at minimal levels, actually worth little in this new time of worldwide high-tech competition. The old wisdom of getting a basic education for every child must fall before the reality that basic education is drastically insufficient in the modern world. American students must as a body sharpen their minds and skills and raise their performance several notches merely to be assured a place in the race. If this tends to emphasize the economic variable, let us quickly note that the growing complexity of the world community requires leaders and citizens who are thoughtful, well informed, and able to deal with complexity.

LEARNING OBJECTIVES

Knowledge Objectives

1 Define education.

2 Distinguish between the functionalist and conflict perspectives of education.

3 Identify the major functions of education in a modern society.

4 Identify some characteristics of American education.

5 Describe the relationship between education and other institutions in society.

6 Identify and describe major problems in education and their relationship to the total society.

Attitudinal Objectives

1 Become more aware of the complex social conditions under which education functions in contemporary U.S. society.

2 Become more aware of the influence of education upon individuals and society.

KEY TERMS

Education   The formal and systematic process which teaches skills and information required to function in society.

Cultural transmission   The process by which values, beliefs, and skills are passed on to the next generation.

Latent functions   Functions which are not intended or official but may become significant to an institution.

Cultural deprivation   A condition in which an individual or a group has not had opportunity to learn important values or skills in a society.

READING ASSIGNMENT

Robertson: *Sociology*, pp. 375–395

READING FOCUS QUESTIONS

1 What is education?

2 What are the characteristics of American education?

3 How does the self-fulfilling prophecy concept relate to education?

4 What are the major differences between the functionalist and conflict perspectives on education?

TV FOCUS QUESTIONS

1 What do Americans expect of education?

2 What are some social problems which come to school on the bus?

3　What are some social conditions in other institutions which affect education?

4　In what ways is education succeeding?

5　In what ways is education failing?

OPTIONAL ACTIVITIES

1　Interview a classroom teacher in junior or senior high school. Ask about classroom conditions which encourage or inhibit good education, along with administrative policies, students' behavior, and parental involvement.

2　Note newspaper articles on education for a week and keep an informal record of the kinds of problems discussed. Are they educational in nature or do they relate to taxes, politics, bureaucracy, or community?

POSTTEST

Multiple Choice

1　As a process, education is similar to
   a. modernization.
   b. socialization.
   c. industrialization.
   d. democratization.

2　The theoretical perspective which emphasizes ways different groups use education as a means of getting power or wealth is
   a. functionalist.
   b. symbolic.
   c. conflict.
   d. integrationist.

3　The educational function which teaches the skills and values society considers important is called
   a. personal development.
   b. social integration.
   c. screening and selection.
   d. cultural transmission.

4　American education is
   a. free and noncompulsory.
   b. non-utilitarian in emphasis.
   c. committed to mass education.
   d. unrelated to social problems.

5 Education relates to other institutions such as family and work in that education

   a. causes problems.

   b. solves problems.

   c. ignores problems.

   d. challenges problems.

6 Serious problems in education, such as drugs, violence, and illiteracy, are

   a. brought to school on the bus.

   b. caused by the failure of education.

   c. school problems, not social problems.

   d. individual problems, not social problems.

POSTTEST ANSWERS

1 b (obj. 1, TV, Text, p. 375)
2 c (obj. 2, Text, p. 380)
3 d (obj. 3, Text, p. 376)
4 c (obj. 4, Text, p. 376)
5 d (obj. 5, TV)
6 a (obj. 6, TV)

Religion in America

19

SOCIOLOGICAL PERSPECTIVE

Americans have always been religious. Symbols of religion abound in our culture. There is the pledge of allegiance to the flag, "in God we trust" on our coins and currency, the Gideon Bible in motel rooms, the cross and steeple on church buildings, and the proliferation of religious programs on television. These and many other symbols and customs remind us of the presence of religion in our culture.

This lesson examines the nature and functions of religion, types of religion, and characteristics of religion in the United States. In particular, it looks at a process called "secularization," the loss of influence of religious beliefs and institutions in a society.

A society that has become increasingly pluralistic, more highly educated, and more pleasure oriented has a changing relationship to traditional religion. Many see it as irrelevant, anti-intellectual, or simply old-fashioned. A part of the process of secularization is the ways in which religion changes to fit the values and preferences of the population. Instead of insisting that people believe and practice the traditional and honored teachings of the church, the church modifies its teachings to fit the times. This process, of course, varies among different types of religious organizations.

Another measure of the loss of influence and respect suffered by traditional religion is the status of religious leaders. Once considered moral leaders of the community, they are now more likely viewed by most citizens as ceremonial leaders, useful primarily at weddings and funerals and as civic club speakers. The power brokers in business and politics at the national or local levels probably have little real respect for the clergy.

On an individual basis, there seems to have been a decrease in the sense of need for institutional religion. Life styles, budgets, entertainment choices and time schedules are all determined with low priority for the church. This reflects a reality pervading the 20th century, an increase of pragmatism, humanism, individualism, and pleasure. Religion is for many an institution to which they pay some respect and offer some involvement but which does not have significant influence in their lives. What is important is family, work, and fun.

Religion is historically a part of the American scene. The great majority of Americans are believers and most of these are monotheistic. The

95

development of the United States has created and sustained a rich mosaic of religion. Its relationship to society is indeed complex. Variables such as individual freedom, anonymity, church membership transfers, private worship, and the electronic church make it very difficult to measure with any precision the real influence of religion in American life. Thus in spite of the process of secularization and apparent loss of influence on the part of institutional religion, the spiritual guest seems still important to many Americans. It has been said that the United States is probably the most religious and the most secular of all societies, a nation with the soul of a church—or perhaps, a nation in search of its soul.

LEARNING OBJECTIVES

Knowledge Objectives

1 Define religion.

2 Describe the sociological approach to religion.

3 Identify the functions of religion.

4 Describe various types of religious organizations.

5 Describe the characteristics of religion in the U.S.

6 Define secularization.

7 Describe some effects of secularization in the U.S.

Attitudinal Objectives

1 Become more aware of the role of religion in your own society and life.

2 Become more aware of the ways in which religion relates to human needs.

KEY TERMS

Religion   A system of beliefs and practices centered on the supernatural.

Monotheism   The belief in one God.

Ecclesia   A form of religious organization which is dominant in a society, claiming the allegiance of most or all of its members.

Denomination   A formally organized, well established religious organization which is one of several such organizations claiming the allegiance of a significant portion of the population.

Sect   A religious organization, informally organized, usually small in relation to denominations, and dogmatic and exclusivistic in teaching and practice.

Cult   A loosely organized religious organization, often centered upon either a particular individual or a certain concept, lacking a comprehensive rationale.

Secularization   The process by which traditional religion loses influence in a society, often by changing its teachings and practices to conform to social trends.

READING ASSIGNMENT

Robertson: *Sociology*, pp. 397–423

READING FOCUS QUESTIONS

1   How does the sociologist approach the study of religion?

2   What are the major types of religion?

3   What are the major functions of religion?

4   What are the four types of religious organizations?

5   What are the characteristics of religion in the United States?

6   What are the major elements in secularization?

TV FOCUS QUESTIONS

1   What are some symbols of religion in the United States?

2   What are some important trends in American religion?

3   What is secularization?

4   Why have many Americans become disillusioned with organized religion?

5   What are some social changes which have affected religion?

OPTIONAL ACTIVITIES

1   Make a list of priorities in your life. Where does religion rank on that list?

2   Talk with a minister, priest, or rabbi who is over 50 and ask about changes in religious teaching and practice over the last 25 years.

POSTTEST

Multiple Choice

1   Religion is best defined as
    a. rituals, prayers, and ceremonies.
    b. churches, crosses, and rosaries.
    c. beliefs and practices related to sacred taboos and superstitions.

2 From the sociological point of view, religion is a product of
   a. superstition.
   b. society.
   c. revelation.
   d. science.

3 Religion relates to society's most important norms in that it
   a. reinforces them.
   b. undermines them.
   c. offers substitutes for them.
   d. generally opposes them.

4 A sect is a religious organization which is
   a. highly organized.
   b. closely identified with denominations.
   c. formal in worship and doctrine.
   d. intolerant of other religious groups.

5 The major characteristic of the *ecclesia* is its
   a. formal worship.
   b. inclusion of most of society.
   c. tolerance of other religious groups.
   d. informal organization.

6 A major characteristic of U.S. religion is its
   a. tradition of formal, established religion.
   b. indifference as to whether or not people are religious.
   c. high degree of tolerance for religious diversity.
   d. lack of public rituals or symbols.

7 The principal cause of secularization in U.S. religion has been the
   a. growing complexity of urban society.
   b. rise of individualism.
   c. decline of interest in science.
   d. weakening of other social institutions.

8 A major effect of secularization in the United States is that
   a. church attendance has declined markedly.
   b. religion now has more influence on individual behavior.
   c. churches have altered their programs to meet daily life needs.
   d. fewer people now profess belief in God.

POSTTEST ANSWERS

1 c (obj. 1, Text, p. 397)
2 b (obj. 2, Text, p. 398)
3 a (obj. 3, Text, p. 401)
4 d (obj. 4, Text, p. 409)
5 b (obj. 4, Text, p. 409)
6 c (obj. 5, Text, p. 412)
7 a (obj. 6, Text, p. 419)
8 c (obj. 7, TV)

20

The Electronic Church

SOCIOLOGICAL PERSPECTIVE

A phenomenon which began its rise to prominence and popularity in the late 1970's and early 1980's is what has been called the"electronic church." It is not really a church in the traditional sense of the term. It is a number of elite organizers and a host of television viewers and supporters. There is no congregation and the members do not sing hymns together. There is broadcast time. There is a mailing list. There is an extensive budget. The electronic church uses television in a special way.

Some churches use television to broadcast their Sunday services or special choral or evangelistic programs, supplementary to their major on-site activities. Electronic churches make television the major medium and thrust of their existence and efforts. They do mass evangelism through television. Funds are raised, communication networks are established, converts are made, and loyalties are created for the electronic church.

Some aspects of this are not new. Many Americans have heard evangelists from Del Rio, Texas, for generations. There is the Lutheran Hour, The Mormon Tabernacle Choir. There was Fulton Sheen with his traditional religious values program. Reverend Ike and his praise of money program is on the other end of the spectrum. Evengelism by radio and television is not new.

What is new is the sophistication and success of the electronic church, that is, the well-dressed image, the psychologically effective appeal, the number of believers, and the quantities of money involved. Electronic churches buy television networks, build medical centers and colleges, and offer 24-hour programming in some metropolitan areas.

In this program we will examine the electronic church as it relates to two of the major recent trends in American religion: the resurgence of evangelicalism and the decline of the role of the intellect, and the accompanying rise of the role of emotionalism and personal experience.

Some electronic churches have erected facilities for worship and other gatherings in the late 1980's. They have built "Christian Disneylands" for family recreation and entertainment. Some programs sell economic success as a basic component of the gospel. These and other changes may be seen as elements in a new stage of development for the electronic church. It is moving from pure electronic status to a more traditional form.

At the same time, traditional mainline churches have begun to make more extensive use of television as a teaching and public relations medium. Thus from a perspective of time and distance, one may observe the profound impact of the electronic church upon the religious scene as a whole.

LEARNING OBJECTIVES

Knowledge Objectives

1 Define fundamentalism and evangelicalism.

2 Define electronic church.

3 Identify and discuss recent trends in U.S. religion.

4 Identify and discuss certain social changes which affect the present status of religion in the United States.

5 Describe the quasi-church nature of the electonic church.

6 Describe the loss of intellect and rise of emotion in the electronic church.

Attitudinal Objective

Become more aware of the role and significance of this form of religion in the lives of many Americans.

KEY TERMS

Electronic church   A religious organization composed of a relatively small number of organizers and a potentially vast number of adherents whose membership is determined by watching television broadcasts.

Evangelicalism   A segment of religion which emphasizes growth through outreach to the unchurched, closely related to fundamentalism.

Fundamentalism   A religious orientation which emphasizes very conservative tenets such as literal authority of scripture, a real heaven and hell, judgment to come, and personal responsibility for sin.

Loss of intellect   A decline in the attention given to a rational understanding of life, religion, and human relationships.

READING ASSIGNMENT

Additional Reading, "American Culture and the Rise of the Electronic Church"

READING FOCUS QUESTIONS

1 What is meant by the cyclical relationship between religion and culture?

2 How have cultural changes affected the function of religion in the United States?

3 What are some basic trends in religion in the United States in recent years?

4 What changes in some church rituals suggest a decline in the role of the intellect and a rise in the role of emotion?

5 What is the electronic church?

6 What are some apparent built-in deficiencies of the electronic church?

7 What seems likely to happen to the electronic church in the future?

TV FOCUS QUESTIONS

1 What is the cyclical relationship between religion and culture?

2 How has modernity affected individuals' need for religion?

3 What trends are apparent in religion in the 1970's and 1980's?

4 What are the major elements of the organization of the electronic church?

5 What social trends contributed to the rise of the electronic church?

6 What are the major deficiences of the electronic church?

OPTIONAL ACTIVITIES

1 Watch a television broadcast of some part of the electronic church for an hour three or four times in a week. Make notes of the program content. What themes can you identify?

2 Visit the worship services of a large, traditional church such as Lutheran or Presbyterian. Visit a church of about the same size which is Baptist, Church of Christ, or Pentecostal. Note the contrast or similarity of worship content and form. What seem to be the major points of emphasis?

POSTTEST

Multiple Choice

1 A significant change in the role of religion in the United States is that more Americans seem to be looking for
   a. heaven.
   b. a better understanding of God.
   c. a sense of belonging.
   d. a place to help others.

2 A belief in the literal truth of the Bible and an emphasis upon outreach to the unchurched is termed
   a. liberalism.
   b. evangelicalism.
   c. Protestantism.
   d. modernism.

3 The major identifying characteristic of the electronic church is that it
  a. has no congregation.
  b. uses television as a medium.
  c. collects money from its members.
  d. teaches the authority of scripture.

4 A major trend in recent U.S. religion is the rise of religious organizations which are
  a. modernistic.
  b. rational.
  c. liberal.
  d. evangelical.

5 The development of U.S. society in terms of technology, industrialization, and pluralism has affected religious activities in that it causes many to seek for
  a. a sense of personal identity.
  b. more assurance of salvation.
  c. increased avenues of service.
  d. a more rational explanation of reality.

6 A decline in the role of the intellect in evangelical religion is indicated by
  a. simplistic solutions to complex problems.
  b. indepth study of sacred writings.
  c. the role of respected theologians.
  d. the formality of worship services.

7 The efforts of many evangelical churches to create an atmosphere of friendliness and individual attention are evidence of the
  a. wisdom of such church leaders.
  b. effectiveness of such activities.
  c. individual search for belonging.
  d. greater sincerity of such groups.

8 The greatest apparent flaw in the electronic church related to its long term effectiveness is the
  a. low skill of its leaders.
  b. lack of community.
  c. lack of appeal to people.
  d. loss of interest in television.

POSTTEST ANSWERS

1	c (obj. 3, TV, Additional Reading)	5	a (obj. 4, Additional Reading)
2	b (obj. 1, TV, Additional Reading)	6	a (obj. 6, TV, Additional Reading)
3	a (obj. 2, TV, Additional Reading)	7	c (obj. 4, Additional Reading)
4	d (obj. 3, TV, Additional Reading)	8	b (obj. 5, TV, Additional Reading)

American Culture and the Rise of the Electronic Church

SOCIAL INSTITUTIONS AND CULTURE

Social institutions such as the family, government, and education are significantly affected by cultural values and changes. The values, technology, and dominant needs of the culture affect all institutions—including religion. There is a complex and pervasive relationship between religion and the culture in which it exists. The relationship is cyclical, that is, religion affects culture which in turn affects religion. From a historical point of view, U.S. culture probably has the greater impact upon religion.

The nature of the religion which people practice is determined by the physical, economic and human relationship conditions under which they live and by the needs which they perceive. Simple societies are heavily dependent upon nature, its cycles and uncertainties. Thus their religion often centers upon gods which control the rain and wind. Their religion pervades their lives and is heavily influential upon their behavior. But its own nature is based upon their perception of the reality and needs which surround their lives.

Modern people are less dependent upon nature but face the discontents and guilt complexes of civilization. Simple people deal with survival needs. Moderns struggle with identity, social relationships, and value judgments. As the culture changes, the religion changes.

CULTURAL CHANGES

Religion once met simple needs for many Americans. It was more "religious" in nature. It dealt with matters of faith: God, heaven, hell, right and wrong. Americans had their struggles for survival in rural, pre-1940 America. Faith was their fortress against despair, death, illness. Now science has become their protection against illness and the elements of nature. But a modern, urban, pluralistic, and individualistic society has cast them adrift from family, community, and a certain sense of self. Thus Americans search for identity, meaning, and purpose in life. For many that search involves religion. And they are looking for much more than answers to the old questions of morality and salvation. Religion must now serve more purposes than in earlier days. Once it provided hope, fortitude, and heaven. Now it must provide focus, meaning, and a sense of identity.

As rapid social change has led to instability and uncertainty in values, Americans have sought answers or escape in various areas. Some have experimented with alcohol, drugs, and sex. Others have tried cultism, "I'm OK, you're OK", and a dozen other fads and gimmicks. Many have turned to the traditional sources of religion for answers. But bureaucratization, depersonalization, and getting lost in the crowd have all had their effects upon religion, as well as education, work, and medicine. Some who turned to traditional churches found them lacking in an adequate response to individual needs. Some who had been in the traditional churches for years or decades also began to sense a need which was not being met.

When such individuals as these, either those inside the churches feeling discontent or those outside looking for religion, began their renewed search for faith, they were not looking so much for heaven as for community, belonging, and emotional security. They were wanting a religion which did for them what family, work, community, and pride in personal achievement no longer did.

TRENDS IN RELIGION

These trends in U.S. culture were accompanied by and probably shared in the stimulation of certain trends in religion. One of these trends is the resurgence, or at least the repopularization, of evangelical religion. Evangelicalism traditionally places great emphasis upon theological teachings which are loosely equated to something called fundamentalism. Fundamentalist theology stresses the authority of scripture, the reality of sin, the coming judgment, heaven and hell, and the divinity of Christ as a personal savior. The God–man relationship is heavily vertical. The individual, personal experience in religion is most significant and ranges from visions of Christ to baptism of the Holy Spirit to narrow escapes from death by fire, accident or cancer. Evangelical churches emphasize a personal God and a close fellowship and love among believers.

Many evangelicals are not fundamentalists. They are liberal in their interpretation and application of the Bible and have a less dogmatic orientation to various social issues of the day such as the role of women in the church, the consumption of alcoholic beverages, and the remarriage of divorced individuals. Those evangelicals who also are essentially fundamentalist, such as the Southern Baptists, are divided into two camps. The most conservative take a narrow and literal view of scripture while the more moderate hold a position which is similar to that of mainline denominations such as Methodists and Presbyterians.

The growth churches in the 1970's and 1980's are all found among the more fundamentalist or conservative types, including Mormons, Southern Baptists, Assemblies of God, Catholics, and certain kinds of Pentecostals.

The majority of electronic churches take a fundamentalist approach to life and religion. Robert Schuler's "Hour of Power" is an exception. Schuler's appeal is to the more educated and affluent. The methodology and content of most electronic religion are aimed at the large working class and the lower-middle class, which is where fundamentalist religion has always had its stronghold in U.S. society.

As the nation turns a bit more religious in the 1980's in terms of church attendance and a growing belief in the importance of religion in life, one would expect the fundamentalists and more conservative evangelical churches to be the growth churches. This may perhaps best be illustrated by asking, "If every family without a new car bought one today, which would most of them buy, a Chevrolet or a Cadillac?" A casual look at the number found in each social class tells us that Baptists and Pentecostals have a much larger pool of potential members in the class structure than do Presbyterians or Unitarians.

A second trend which seems apparent is the decline of the role of the intellect in popular religion, accompanied by a growing emphasis upon subjective, emotional experiences. This balance in religious experience is not new, having been dominant in several American religious organizations throughout their history. What is new is the growing popularity of such churches and the impact of this trend upon mainline churches in the U.S. Both Catholic and Protestant churches have historically based their faith upon a systematic theology with historic roots. Their statements of faith were comprehensive, intellectually respectable, and characterized by continuity.

An obvious and significant change in Catholic ritual occurred when Mass was celebrated in English in 1965. Changes in Protestant ritual have been more subtle but nonetheless quite significant, and although not limited to evangelical churches, are more pronounced there. Two changes seem most obvious and significant. These are in the music and in the general atmosphere of the worship. The music has been popularized and made even less formal than that which once characterized many of these churches. Its major sources seem to be camp songs for teenagers and country-western models in music, along with some influence from black spirituals. There is a conspicuous decline in the frequency of use of traditional hymns. It is more highly personalized and, if possible, more emotional in content.

The general atmosphere of the worship has moved a few notches past the revival meeting on the scale of informality and presumed spontaneity. In earlier times and in more simple American communities, church-goers greeted each other at church with spontaneity and friendliness born of the nature of their community. They really did know each other. Their greetings were natural and unplanned. In modern, urban churches—especially when memberships number several hundreds or even thousands—people do not know each other. Yet many individuals come to church to find friendliness and personal attention. In keeping with the bureaucratization of our times, many churches have created friendliness and spontaneity in the form of what is loosely called the "love feast."

Before this ritual, a church official announces, "This is a friendly church and we all love each other." All individuals present rise to greet each other, shake hands or embrace, and generally chat about life and God or the weather. Reviews of this ritual are mixed. Some individuals believe that it evidences friendliness and are warmed by it. Others have already greeted friends or pew companions and sense a high degree of artificiality in the ritual. In any event, the myth of church friendliness survives and another attempt has been made to cause individuals to feel that they belong. Such rituals may well be more of a testimony to the awareness of church leaders that friendliness is important than an exercise with lasting effects.

THE ELECTRONIC CHURCH

A religious form which most closely exemplifies the decline in the role of the intellect and the rise of emotion and individualism is the electronic church. Actually a quasi-church, the electronic church has no congregation, no gatherings on Sunday, and no love feasts. It is a number of highly organized groups of individuals who broadcast religious and semi-religious content on television. Its membership is a mailing list of individuals who write for prayer or guidance or in support of the program content—and who give money. Highly evangelical in nature, the electronic church also reaches out to individuals with personal needs, both on the broadcast and in later phone and letter contacts. The number of individuals who respond to the electronic church seems an eloquent testimony to the high level of loneliness and need for personal attention in many sectors of U.S. society today.

The electronic church, similar to many real evangelical churches discussed earlier, is characterized by a neglect of systematic theology and historical intellectual concerns. There is a serious oversimplification of issues, needs, and solutions. The message is unidimensional: "God loves you. Place your trust in Jesus and everything will be all right with your life." The validity of the message is supported by scripture references. It is highlighted by personal testimony, frequently that of a celebrity of some kind—a movie star, an ex-drug addict, a rich business man, a rock queen, politician, or an ex-convict.

There is a strong emphasis on the "born again" experience, charismatic gifts of healing and other miracles. Some of the settings, both on stage and in churches, differ little in atmosphere and methodology from the musical concerts which attract and influence fans through carefully designed music and motions, loudness, repetition, color, lights—all of which appeal much to emotions and senses and little to intelligence or rationality.

Many Americans, disillusioned with traditional churches, dropped out over the last three decades. It may be from among these that the electronic church draws many of its converts. A quite attractive aspect of the electronic church for some is undoubtedly the simplicity and ease of joining: a hand on the TV while the minister prays for you, a letter requesting a prayer or a tract or whatever formula is being used—all from the comfort of one's easy chair with remote control TV. There is no attendance, no dress code, no group prayer—only a TV set and the telephone.

It is interesting to speculate upon the demographic characteristics of adherents to the electronic church. We know that about two-thirds of them are already churchgoers, age 55 and above, female, and that many of them live in the Bible Belt. We know that membership in traditional churches which share the major tenets of the electronic church comes from the lower half of the social class structure. Thus it is not surprising that the broadcasts of the electronic church and worship services of other churches in the evangelical form should be low on intellect and high on emotion.

SOME CONCLUSIONS AND FORECASTS

The detached, scientific observer may well conclude that the electronic church has serious built-in deficiencies. It is probably too emotional, too individualistic, and too easy to join. It does not in itself create community among believers. It greatly oversimplifies both life and religion. In a broader sense, one must question whether those converts to an emotion-based religion—whether electronic or otherwise—who are urban and exposed to real life complexities on a daily basis can long sustain a significant part of their life-experience with their emotions in control and their minds turned off.

Whatever deficiencies of mainline churches drive people to the electronic church, or its more traditionally organized counterparts, it may be that after a sojourn in what will be for many a foreign land psychologically, they will return to the familiar terrain of the middle American denominations. Or, of perhaps equal probability, the new evangelicals may become more traditional and less emotional as the new wears off. There is little reason for us to expect a search for meaning to be resolved any more satisfactorily in a religion with its mind turned off than in other mindless pursuits of however less noble origin.

In a society as pluralistic and varied as the United States, as technological and industralized, it seems unlikely that any more than a small but significant portion of the population will ever be converted to the electronic church. The only thing new about it is the electronics. More traditional churches are adapting content and methodology to meet social and psychological needs. They have buildings, real people, and they are in the community.

As to the non-electronic versions of the new evangelicalism, we must conclude that since they have been around for such a long time, they are very likely to survive among basically the same population which they have always served. It seems unlikely that they will make significant and lasting inroads into the membership of other traditional churches whose more intelligent and comprehensive approach to life and religion and whose history of dealing with complex issues may see them through these times of change to a rebirth of relevance and vitality.

21

Government

SOCIOLOGICAL PERSPECTIVE

The gist of this lesson is an examination of contemporary attitudes toward government. Much of our lives is dominated by large organizations: the factory, county hospital, the school district, city hall, national television networks, Exxon, General Motors, and the large church. Everywhere we turn with our needs, we face large, impersonal, unyielding organizations. The largest of these is the federal government.

We resent government more than other large organizations because its influence is so broad and pervasive. It tells us where to send our kids to school, how warm the bedroom can be in winter, how fast we can drive on our expensive super highways, and whether or not to drink diet cola.

Complex issues abound in American society today. Most of us do not understand trade deficits, oil depletion allowances, Eurodollars or Federal Reserve policies. We know that taxes are high and going higher, energy is becoming critical, crime is worse, and we can't afford a new house. We feel a sense of being trapped and powerless—and we blame a lot of this condition upon those in government who are supposed to be managing those complex issues.

Many Americans have lost faith in the government's ability or will to deal effectively with pressing national issues. A condition prevails which is called "alienation." This is a sense, a feeling, a perception of being separated from something of value: God, family, community, work. This lesson hypothesizes that a new strain of alienation arose in the late sixties and early seventies—a strain which is more virulent. The elusive, intangible nature of alienation makes its significance easily missed or underrated. It is not just that people are lonely, afraid, angry, or cynical. It is not just the complexity, impersonalization, and bureaucracy of large organizations. It is the perception that nothing can be done about the problems which plague us. It is the fatalism, despair, and lack of hope. A poll in the late seventies showed that for the first time in American history, a majority of Americans believed that their children's lives would be worse than their lives are.

This lesson examines the nature and extent of alienation from government, as well as the "no-win" situation which may characterize government today. It also takes a hopeful look at what may be done to improve the future.

LEARNING OBJECTIVES

Knowledge Objectives

1 Describe Weber's three types of legitimate authority.

2 Distinguish between the functionalism and the conflict approach to explaining the American power structure.

3 Define "power elite" as it relates to U.S. society.

4 Define alienation.

5 Describe alienation as it relates to government today.

6 Identify three dimensions of alienation.

7 Explain the "no-win" situation of government.

8 Identify proposals for improving attitudes toward government.

Attitudinal Objectives

1 Develop a greater awareness of how one's own life is influenced by government and, in turn, of why one's attitudes toward government are what they are.

2 Develop a greater awareness and appreciation of the complexity of the task facing government.

KEY TERMS

Alienation   A perception or feeling of being separated from something of value, such as God, family, community or work.

Charismatic   A type of authority based upon perceived personal qualities of a leader, such as wisdom, courage, dedication, or power.

Functionalist   A perspective which holds that various elements in a society exist and operate to maintain the system and meet social needs.

Conflict   A perspective which holds that social conditions exist and continue based upon the power of the "have's" and the weakness of the "have-not's."

READING ASSIGNMENT

Robertson: *Sociology*, pp. 479–503

READING FOCUS QUESTIONS

1 What are the three major types of legitimate authority?

2 What is the functionalist approach to understanding the state?

3 What is the conflict approach to understanding the state?

4 What are the major elements in the American political process?

5 Who are the power elite in American society?

TV FOCUS QUESTIONS

1 What is alienation?

2 What are the three major dimensions of alienation as it affects participation in government?

3 In what sense is there a "new strain" of alienation in American society?

4 How does alienation affect individual behavior in areas other than political participation?

5 In what sense is the government in a "no-win" situation?

6 What are some proposals for improving the relationship of citizens to government?

OPTIONAL ACTIVITIES

1 Check the major news stories in a paper for one week. Note the complexity of issues facing the federal government and the diversity of interests groups seeking a hearing, support, or changes.

2 Ask ten people if they trust the federal government. Ask why or why not.

POSTTEST

Multiple Choice

1 Weber's three types of legitimate authority include all *except*
   a. charismatic.
   b. traditional.
   c. functional.
   d. bureaucratic.

2 A point of view which emphasizes power as being used to safeguard the interests of the privileged.
   a. functionalist
   b. conflict
   c. bureaucratic
   d. traditional

3   The "power elite" concept as held by C.W. Mills suggests that
   a. a few powerful individuals have conspired to dominate society.
   b. individuals of similar social background in positions of power in government, industry, and the military cooperate in policy making.
   c. although some men are very powerful, the masses have great influence on high level decisions.
   d. there is a wide distribution and random sampling of the population in the power circles of society.

4   Alienation is
   a. a feeling of separation from something important to the individual.
   b. an objective evaluation of reality, concluding that conditions are bad.
   c. a new problem in American society.
   d. related only to government.

5   Alienation from government is best expressed by
   a. "Ah, I still have confidence in 'em."
   b. "Ah, I wouldn't trust too many of them too much for the most part."
   c. "Well, just too much bureaucracy."
   d. "Everywhere you look, the government has their hands in it."

6   The main dimensions of alienation include all *except*
   a. distrust.
   b. a sense of powerlessness.
   c. a sense of meaninglessness.
   d. a belief that conditions will improve.

7   Government is in a "no-win" situation because
   a. qualified individuals cannot be found to work in government.
   b. the job of President is too big for any man.
   c. so many diverse groups have expectations of government that helping one hurts the other.
   d. bureaucracy is basically inefficient.

8   Proposals for reducing the amount of alienation toward government include all *except*
   a. a period of national service for all young people.
   b. a renewed emphasis upon citizenship responsibilities as well as rights.
   c. a continued encouragement of individualism and hedonism.
   d. lowering expectations of government and society.

POSTTEST ANSWERS

1	c	(obj. 1, Text, p. 481)	5	b	(obj. 5, TV)
2	b	(obj. 2, Text, p. 485)	6	d	(obj. 6, TV)
3	b	(obj. 3, Text, p. 496)	7	c	(obj. 7, TV)
4	a	(obj. 4, TV)	8	c	(obj. 8, TV)

22

The Work Ethic

SOCIOLOGICAL PERSPECTIVE

Would you take a garden hoe to the field at 7:00 A.M. and begin chopping weeds from corn along half-mile rows for minimum wages? You must not look around much or lean on the hoe handle. There is no water to drink until you work a round trip. There is an hour for lunch and then back to the field until 6:00 P.M. There are no fringe benefits such as Muzak, union, or sick leave. There is no promotion.

Some of your fathers and most of your grandfathers had such experiences at work. So did many American women. So do some workers today. But most do not. Most would walk away from such jobs as unnecessary, contemptible, or for someone else.

This lesson examines the work experience and workers' attitudes toward their work, along with some consequences for American society.

The essence of the work ethic is that individuals will work hard to survive, to get ahead, or to obtain what they want in life. The idea that people will work hard if the job is satisfying, fulfilling, or creative is not part of the work ethic concept. In these two thoughts we may find expressed the essential change which has occurred in American attitudes toward work in the past few decades. Americans who worked the farms, coal mines, and factories in the first half of this century worked in conditions which included boredom, physical exhaustion, isolation, low pay, no chance for advancement, and little control over any of these. Their lives centered on work because of the very long hours it consumed and the necessity of doing it for economic survival.

With technological advances and increased affluence, the American work force found leisure time and resources to focus their lives on something other than boring but necessary jobs. Hours were shorter. Pay was better. Conditions improved. Taking for granted the possession of considerably more than subsistence resources, the American worker began to seek other rewards in work. Work should be meaningful, fulfilling, and creative. There should be intrinsic rewards to the job itself. And, in fact, thus it is with a greater number of workers today, although many workers still find drudgery, boredom, and meaninglessness in their workday.

A major variable which has contributed to the decline of the work ethic is the massive welfare program which has been in place now for several decades. The "welfare floor," as it has been called, is just high enough to make the pursuit of a minimum-wage job not very attractive, especially if one has little ambition or several children to manage. The high pay scales to which American workers in many areas become accustomed make workers unwilling to take lower-paying jobs when their high-paying jobs fail. Unions have until recent years been able to protect workers in mass whose productivity and quality of work were quite low by historical and worldwide standards. This meant in effect that it was not the hard work that made individuals prosper, but the political agreements worked out between labor and management.

The 1980's brought dramatic changes to the world marketplace for goods and labor. Foreign labor and production made foreign goods more competitive than U.S.-made goods. Advancing U.S. technology in computers and robotics gave industry the power to replace human workers. Until the early 1960's, a high school graduate or dropout could go to work at union wages for GM, Ford, or the steel mill. New jobs in those areas have been gone in the United States for about two decades now. They have been replaced by jobs in the fast food industry which are non-union, low-paying, and non-macho.

This places high priority and a real urgency on the matter of post-high-school education for American youth. Although there were no promotions on the assembly lines on which their fathers and grandfathers (and some grandmothers) worked, they were union, well paid, and had protection and pride in the picture. "See that Ford, son? I made the transmission on it!" A man could flex his muscles over that. "Well, son, your old man makes the best french fries in town!" somehow just doesn't have quite the same ring.

The work ethic is on its way back, but getting there is going to be traumatic in the training, adjustments, and mind-set changes that must take place in American workers. They will also have the fat American industrial bureaucracy to contend with. American industry, so far, is trying to compete with foreign car makers by extending the warranties. Ross Perot has a different idea. He would go into the GM paint shop and say to the workers, "Why can't you guys paint a car as well as the Japanese?"

LEARNING OBJECTIVES

Knowledge Objectives

1 Define division of labor.

2 Define work ethic and review its history in U.S. society.

3 Explain what is meant by worker alienation and anomie.

4 Distinguish between capitalism and socialism as ways of producing and distributing goods and services.

5 Distinguish between mechanical and organic solidarity and describe U.S. society in those terms.

6 Discuss some of the social effects of modernization.

Attitudinal Objectives

1 Become more aware of and appreciate more fully the role of work in life and society.

2 Become more aware of the effect of your own work and your attitude toward it upon other aspects of your life.

KEY TERMS

Work ethic   The idea that hard work is necessary and useful to survival and success, combined with a willingness to perform on the job for these reasons.

Division of labor   A specialization in work roles created by the needs and values of a society, greatly affected by the level of technology in that society.

Alienation   A feeling of separation from any institution or process, resulting in a sense of meaningless and powerlessness in one's participation.

Protestant ethic   The foundation of the American work ethic, with origins in early Protestantism which stressed the signs of grace attached to success in work.

Modernization   The process of economic and social change stimulated by the technology of industrialization.

READING ASSIGNMENT

Robertson: *Sociology,* pp. 451–475

READING FOCUS QUESTIONS

1 What is the division of labor?

2 What is alienation and how does it relate to American work today?

3 What are the differences between capitalism and socialism?

4 What are some social effects of modernization in the United States?

TV FOCUS QUESTIONS

1 What is work?

2 What purposes does work serve?

3 What is the Protestant Ethic?

4 How has the nature of work changed in the United States?

5 What are the sources of changes in the work ethic?

OPTIONAL ACTIVITIES

1 Write a description of the jobs at which you have worked and are now working. Note which aspects of the jobs interest you most or are most rewarding.

2   Ask a few people who work if they would prefer to have their jobs more specialized or broadened to include a greater variety of tasks and more widespread contact with people.

POSTTEST

Multiple Choice

1   The division of labor is more highly specialized in societies which are
   a. hunting and gathering.
   b. agricultural.
   c. low industrialized.
   d. high industrialized.

2   Durkheim said that modern societies are held together by
   a. mechanical solidarity.
   b. organic solidarity.
   c. religious solidarity.
   d. community solidarity.

3   The idea that hard work is necessary in seeking God's grace is found in the
   a. work ethic.
   b. Protestant ethic.
   c. American dream.
   d. frontier spirit.

4   Alienation from work in Marx's theory means that
   a. work is too hard.
   b. pay is too low.
   c. work is exploitative.
   d. work is too easy.

5   The ideas of personal profit and free competition are found in the ideology of
   a. communism.
   b. socialism.
   c. capitalism.
   d. democratic socialism.

6   The social effects of the process of modernization are felt
   a. primarily in the family.
   b. in a few of the basic institutions.
   c. largely in the area of work.
   d. in virtually every area of society.

7 In U.S. society today, workers are motivated
   a. by a wide range of social and economic factors.
   b. largely by the need to survive economically.
   c. by religious and moral factors.
   d. by a search for personal identity.

8 The major change in the work ethic over the past few decades is that workers are
   a. working much harder for success.
   b. less alienated from their work.
   c. seeking more satisfaction in work.
   d. more conscious of society's needs.

POSTTEST ANSWERS

1 d (obj. 1, Text, p. 453)
2 b (obj. 5, Text, p. 454)
3 b (obj. 2, TV)
4 c (obj. 3, Text, p. 457)
5 c (obj. 4, Text, p. 460)
6 d (obj. 6, Text, p. 473)
7 a (obj. 2, TV)
8 c (obj. 2, TV)

23

Sports

It is the end of the day. About 20 African men of various ages gather in a local hut to drink homemade beer—served, of course, by a local wench. In London, upper middle class businessmen and executives drink beer quietly in a pub and discuss the market. Across town, working class men loudly drink beer and throw darts for an hour or so before heading home to the family and evening meal. In the southern United States, a bass boat moves slowly and quietly across a small lake toward Joe and Harry's favorite fishing spot. They will miss supper and the kids' bedtime, but the fish are waiting. In East St. Louis, the steel workers spend an hour at Ed's Tavern drinking beer—then off to home and another one before supper. In Dallas, it's already 7:00 in the evening, but it is summer and Bill is off with his company's slow-pitch softball team for an evening of play and beer. The loser buys the beer. In any event, Bill's wife can watch awhile and go home early with the kids, or just stay home. How long has it been since you got away from it all?

The scene is the Roman Coliseum, *circa* A.D. 90. As a pre-game show, prelude to the real contest of the day when professional gladiators engage in to-the-death combat for the pleasure of the Emperor and the populace, a number of unarmed, humiliated, and helpless individuals of both sexes and various ages are crowded to the center of the arena. There they await the attack of hungry animals to the delight of a packed stadium of individuals who have rationalized that Christians are less than human and deserve to die. The scene changes to early New England as crowds gather for the witch-burning. God and truth will be vindicated; the community will be unified against evil. And it will be entertained. In the old west an entire town turns out for the hanging—or lynching—of a wrongdoer. Today he meets his Maker. And something exciting has happened in our town. It is the late 1970's and Reggie Jackson has hit three home runs in one game and becomes the most valuable player of the series. He is running for his life through a mob of fans who have taken over the field. Helmeted police are attacked with everything from Red Delicious apples to two-by-fours hurled from the stands. Bases are ripped up, turf is destroyed, beer bottles are flying. At third base, a fan is on the ground, bleeding from a head wound while other fans continue to kick and punch him. How long has it been since you saw something exciting?

At different times and places in history and in various societies, humans have had their play, games, fun, and recreation in many ways. The classic purposes of sports include recreation, exercise, diversion from work, and community unification. All of these functions endure in our time. In this lesson we will, among other things, note two particular realities in American sports. First, there is a significant increase in participation (especially if we count spectator sports) and second, the level of violence, hedonism, and escape from reality is noticeably increasing. Sport is assuming an increasingly important role in American life. It excites us. It produces most of our heroes. It consumes more of our time and money than ever before.

This lesson raises and examines serious questions about sports. What is the relationship between culture and sports? What social conditions stimulate the growing popularity of sports and the intensity of both participants and spectators? Can baseball really be made as interesting and violent as football by making the "safe" and "out" signals more violent? What are the human needs which drive people to such extremes in sports?

The role of sports in public education and higher education came under very close scrutiny in the mid-1980's. Public educators in many states became aware of the inconsistency and failure of policies and programs which graduated students who could not function at a basic level of literacy yet had been extensively involved in sports and other extracurricular activities. "No-pass, no-play" became the operational phrase for education reform. The NCAA raised entry standards in academics for athletes and cracked down on cheating by players and coaches.

In another public sector, professional sports issues such as drug abuse, salaries, and city economics received a much closer look. Howard Cosell wrote a book in which he popularized the concept of the "Sports Syndrome," which calls attention to some serious fallacies and myths perpetuated by the NFL and some sports writers and speakers.

LEARNING OBJECTIVES

Knowledge Objectives

1 Describe sport as a sociological phenomenon.

2 Identify the classic functions of sport in society.

3 Identify the nature and extent of American participation in sports.

4 Examine some major dysfunctions of sports.

5 Identify ways in which the nature of sport in a society reflects its values.

6 Examine the need which people have for heroes and conditions which cause most heroes to rise today from sports.

Attitudinal Objectives

1 To become more aware of the significant role of sports in American culture.

2 To appreciate more fully the extent to which many individuals depend upon sports to escape from boredom, find identity and express their feelings and values.

KEY TERMS

Sport   A competitive physical activity regulated by established rules.

Microcosm   A small universe or world which embodies the realities and relationships of a larger world in which it exists.

Spectator sport   One in which professionals engage for money and are observed by non-participants, usually for a fee.

Participant-oriented sport   One in which individuals engage without pay for purposes such as exercise, socializing, or pleasure.

READING ASSIGNMENT

Robertson: *Sociology*, pp. 95–100

READING FOCUS QUESTIONS

1 What are some indications of the importance of sports in American society?

2 How have changes in the economic institution affected sports?

3 Who benefits from the wealth generated by the sports industry?

4 What is the relationship between sport and American values?

5 How are race, class, and sexual status related to sports?

TV FOCUS QUESTIONS

1 In what sense is sport a sociological phenomenon?

2 Describe the extent of Americans' involvement in sport.

3 What are some primary motivations which individuals have for becoming involved in sport?

4 What are some negative aspects of sport today?

5 How does sport unify a nation or a community?

6 Why do we find most of our heroes today in sports?

OPTIONAL ACTIVITIES

1 Examine the hypothesis that watching sports events on television is addictive or compulsive behavior for some individuals. Monitor your own time use for two weekends and count the actual hours spent in watching sports.

2 Collect data on sports violence and injuries and on pending or proposed legal measures to manage sports violence. Ask a few sports fans what they think about those measures.

POSTTEST

Multiple Choice

1 Sport is a sociological phenomenon because it is
   a. violent.
   b. physical.
   c. expensive.
   d. social.

2 Traditional functions of sport include all *except*
   a. exercise and recreation.
   b. escape from responsibility.
   c. unification of community.
   d. providing corporate income and educational funds.

3 The percentage of Americans who say they participate daily in some form of physical exercise is about
   a. 10%.
   b. 30%.
   c. 50%.
   d. 80%.

4 The difference between a healthy involvement in sport and an involvement which is dysfunctional is
   a. the kind of sport one chooses.
   b. the extent of involvement relative to other life elements.
   c. whether the sport is participant or spectator.
   d. whether the sport is individual or group structured.

5 Sport reflects the values of a society in that
   a. the power structure in sports is similar to that in society.
   b. attitudes toward race, sex, wealth change in sports.
   c. people's values change when they participate in sports.
   d. a clear priority is placed upon important values such as education, morality, and fair play.

6 People look to sports for heroes today because
   a. athletes are the most superior individuals around.
   b. sports are the only place where glamour and excitement may be found.
   c. they are cynical about government, religion, and other traditional sources of heroes.
   d. unlike other social institutions, sports has escaped corruption and abuse.

POSTTEST ANSWERS

1 d (obj. 1, TV)
2 d (obj. 2, TV)
3 c (obj. 3, TV)
4 b (obj. 4, TV)
5 a (obj. 5, TV)
6 c (obj. 6, TV)

Social Processes and Change

24

Crowd Behavior

SOCIOLOGICAL PERSPECTIVE

This lesson focuses upon crowd behavior, its origin, nature, and effect. It takes as an example the California gas lines of 1979. It presents some generalizations about the present status of American society in terms of urbanism, dependence upon oil technology, our love affair with the auto as symbolic of individual freedom and mobility, and the state of affairs in human relationships among strangers. An old phenomenon which seems to be emerging with fresh vitality is what occurs when someone yells, "Fire." It may be observed when two people claim the same parking spot in a shopping center, when the crowd exits the stadium after the game, or when a casual freeway exit maneuver brings on an encounter with a nut.

California, as well as much of urban America, is characterized by high geographic mobility, rapid change in population, and increase in size and density of population. Perhaps most significantly, the make-up of the population has become very heterogeneous, that is, people differ greatly from each other in many ways: state of origin, type of work, religion, level of education, family values. The rapid growth of the state for the past two decades or so has eroded many traditional values. Rapid change and high mobility have encouraged very high individualism.

The sunshine, high wages, low tradition, and Hollywood influence have combined to create a highly hedonistic, self-centered culture. Los Angeles, for example, lacks identity as a city. It has been called "a lot of suburbs searching for a city." There is much sociological significance to this type of urban setting. Community is hard to create and sustain. Nearness to beach, mountains, the freeway system, and the pleasure motif combine to turn a lot of people into pleasure seekers.

Nationwide, complex organizations have such influence and power and are viewed with such cynicism and distrust, that the total society is set up for panic when a real problem occurs—such as an apparently severe energy shortage. There is no trusted institution or individual to whom people can turn for information and guidance. Big oil, state and federal government, GM, and the media do not inspire confidence. The total picture is one which is filled with symptoms relating to potential collective (crowd) behavior.

Californians were in the forefront of inflation—housing, autos, and other living costs escalated first in California, matched only perhaps by New York.

High living Californians were accustomed to good wages, sunshine, and low energy costs for autos and homes. The number of autos increased more rapidly in California in the 1970's than in any other state, and the typical distances traveled to work, or to after-work or weekend entertainment and recreation increased.

Other concerns ranged from famous L.A. smog to San Francisco panther snipers, to the influence of conservative religion and politics. Like other regions of the nation, California has its share of family disorganization in the form of divorce, living together, and child care problems in two-income families. In addition, there were the mud slides, then the droughts with forest fires, burned homes, and water shortages. People with $100 water bills, bricks in their toilet tanks, dirty Mercedes Benz's with empty tanks, and half-way through divorces are in no mood for long gas lines.

The minor gas crunch of 1973 was probably long forgotten when the spring of 1979 came to California. International events involving Iran, OPEC, and Japan have a way of not being noticed by beautiful, busy people on the way to the beach. They were driving a little farther to work each year, traffic was a bit heavier, gas a bit higher. One day, a station attendant said, "Sorry, we're out of low-lead." The response was probably, "You knew you were going to open today, didn't you?!" and on to another station. But overnight the other stations closed and lines began forming at all open stations. Literally, before anyone could focus on what was happening, the lines were there.

When individuals are faced with near-empty gas tanks in vehicles upon which they are so dependent in their daily activities, when the gas lines are long and getting longer, and, most importantly, when there are no answers from any source as to causes or solutions, they feel a sense of being trapped by forces beyond their control. While the pressure is building toward some kind of action, many individuals suspect strongly that big oil is conspiring to raise prices through scarcity and that big government is ineptly making the situation worse through allocation regulations. They learn that the federal energy department is increasing its own gas consumption almost 30% a year through bureaucratic growth and idling engines. These suspicions, founded or unfounded, add to the sense of anger and frustration felt by many in the gas lines—and make them highly susceptible to the idea that one ought to do something, anything!

LEARNING OBJECTIVES

Knowledge Objectives

1 Define collective behavior.

2 Identify various types of crowds.

3 Describe various characteristics of crowds.

4 Describe two theories of crowd behavior.

5 Describe sources of instability in U.S. society which may contribute to crowd behavior.

6 Evaluate the role of media in the gas crisis of 1979.

Attitudinal Objectives

1 Become more aware of one's own vulnerability to participation in crowd behavior and of the sources contributing to it.

2 Become more aware of the impact of social psychological variables upon individual behavior.

KEY TERMS

Collective behavior The spontaneous activity of a relatively large number of people.

Crowd A relatively large number of people gathered for temporary purposes in a temporary setting.

Emergent norms theory The idea that new norms develop during crowd behavior which guide and justify that behavior.

READING ASSIGNMENT

Robertson: *Sociology*, pp. 533–551

READING FOCUS QUESTIONS

1 What is collective behavior?

2 What basic conditions must exist to make collective behavior possible?

3 What is a crowd?

4 What are the characteristics of crowds?

5 What are two major theories of crowd behavior?

TV FOCUS QUESTIONS

1 What is collective behavior?

2 When is crowd behavior likely to occur?

3 What are some built-in sources of crowd behavior in the United States today?

4 What are the dynamics of crowd behavior?

5 What contributed to the gas crisis in California in 1979?

6 What accounts for the unusual behavior of people in the gas lines?

7 What was the role of the media in the gas lines crisis?

8 What is the likelihood that crowd behavior will become more frequent and intense?

OPTIONAL ACTIVITIES

1 See if you can recall any situations in which you have been involved which qualify for the description of crowd behavior (perhaps an accident scene, long theater lines, or an incident at a football game). Compare the factors in those situations to the factors examined in this lesson.

2 Ask a few people about their experiences or observations related to the behavior of crowds.

POSTTEST

Multiple Choice

1 Collective behavior is
   a. any group engaged in an activity.
   b. a number of people watching a fire.
   c. a relatively large number of people engaged in spontaneous activity.
   d. two people arguing about a football score.

2 Types of crowds include
   a. casual and expressive.
   b. formal and informal.
   c. violent and non-violent.
   d. a and c.

3 Most crowds
   a. vary in character but have some characteristics in common.
   b. have little in common in terms of their nature.
   c. are alike in almost every way.
   d. differ very little from other collections of people such as work groups or social gatherings.

4 The emergent norms theory holds that
   a. crowd behavior can be analyzed in terms of ordinary social and psychological processes.
   b. basic norms actually emerge more completely during crowd behavior.
   c. crowd behavior can be explained only by a totally different approach to examining norms.
   d. basic norms evolve during crowd behavior and become a permanent part of the normative system.

5 Conditions in U.S. society which may contribute to certain kinds of crowd behavior include

   a. general affluence and fulfilled expectations.

   b. social equality and economic prosperity.

   c. social instability and a sense of powerlessness.

   d. a high level of mutual identification and a sense of solidarity in population.

6 One of the most common experiences of people in a crowd is

   a. a growth in confidence in authority figures.

   b. an emotional urgency compelling them to act.

   c. an identification with the crowd members which stimulates selflessness.

   d. an increase in the dominance of rational processes.

7 One source of frustration contributing to crowd behavior in the 1979 gas line crisis was the

   a. feeling that there just wasn't any gas to be sold.

   b. sense that individuals had not expressed their feelings to government.

   c. feeling that Americans have less and less control over their lives in general.

   d. early warnings of 1973 which caused many to prepare for a later crisis.

8 Observers of the gas line crisis of 1979 felt that generally the media

   a. reported in a responsible manner throughout the crisis.

   b. had little effect either during the early or later part of the crisis.

   c. were primarily responsible for the panic buying.

   d. sensationalized the problem in early stages, contributing to a self-fulfilling prophecy effect.

POSTTEST ANSWERS

   1 c (obj. 1, TV, Text, p. 533)
   2 d (obj. 2, Text, p. 539)
   3 a (obj. 3, Text, p. 537)
   4 a (obj. 4, Text, p. 539)
   5 c (obj. 5, TV)
   6 b (obj. 4, TV)
   7 c (obj. 5, TV)
   8 d (obj. 6, TV)

25

Social Movements

SOCIOLOGICAL PERSPECTIVE

Social movements usually reflect or indicate trouble spots in a society—some issue or segment of the population which is neglected or treated unfairly. They are functional in that they provide a safety valve for pressures which, if not expressed in this way, could be expressed in other ways much more destructive to society, without improving conditions. There is typically a lot of waste and hurt in the origin and evolution of a social movement. Pioneers are martyrs. Polemics are inevitable. Movements do not arise about minor issues.

The essence of a movement's objectives is frequently blurred or lost in the heat of polemics and the politics of personalities. Stereotypes, assumptions, reaction, prejudice, and exaggeration are the companions of social movements and are likely to be in bed with those for the movement as well as those against the movement. Social movements are not made in heaven. But they tend always to be seen as utterly righteous by their proponents. This righteousness is perceived as arrogance by those not as enthusiastic about the cause, whether it is women's rights, spiritual gifts in church, or save the whales campaigns.

When the dust and rhetoric of the movement have settled and life returns to normal, it is, in American society at least, always a somewhat different kind of normal. Adjustments have been made in various social relationships, new alliances have been formed, and some rules have been changed. Almost inevitably, some progress has been achieved for some sector of the population—often at what may seem to be a loss for some other sector. It may be years or even decades before the total effect of a social movement can be accurately assessed.

LEARNING OBJECTIVES

Knowledge Objectives

1 Define social movement.

2 List three characteristics of social movements.

3 Identify four stages through which social movements typically develop.

4 Identify several social conditions which typically give rise to social movements.

5 Identify the social forces during the fifties and sixties which stimulated the women's movement.

6 Identify ways in which the role of women has changed as a result of the the women's movement.

Attitudinal Objectives

1 Develop a better understanding and appreciation of conditions which give rise to social movements, and thus of the motivation of those involved in the movements.

2 Develop a more objective attitude toward social movements of various kinds, whether you favor or oppose a particular movement.

KEY TERMS

Social movement The cooperative efforts of a rather large number of people or groups either to bring about certain change in society or to resist some change.

Institutional discrimination A form of unfair treatment to individuals or groups which is built into the social system and its institutions, a general feature of the society.

Sexism An ideology or belief system which assumes that sexual inequalities exist and are based upon biology, and which varies expectations, rights, and behavior according to sex.

READING ASSIGNMENT

Robertson: *Sociology*, pp. 552–563

READING FOCUS QUESTIONS

1 What are some examples of social movements in history?

2 What is the "strain" theory of social movements?

3 What are the major characteristics of social movements?

4 What is the relationship between social movements and social problems?

5 What are the stages through which social movements typically pass?

TV FOCUS QUESTIONS

1 What are some ways in which females have experienced discrimination?

2 What is a social movement?

3 What are three major characteristics of social movements?

4 What are the four stages of development of most social movements?

5 What were the social forces during the fifties and sixties which stimulated the women's movement?

6 How has the role of women changed as a result of the women's movement?

OPTIONAL ACTIVITIES

1 Ask five males and five females under 30 and the same number over 40 what they think about the women's movement. Compare your answers.

2 Make a list of 20 jobs or professions which have some direct bearing upon your own life or with which you come into direct contact. Write beside each item on the list the sex of those who usually occupy the job. Consider how you would react personally if the sex of those occupying each job was different from what you wrote on the list.

POSTTEST

Multiple Choice

1 All of these are examples of social movements *except*
   a. civil rights.
   b. ERA.
   c. gay liberation.
   d. energy crisis.

2 A major characteristic of social movements is that they usually
   a. begin with a large gathering of people in a public forum.
   b. are very narrow in the methods they employ.
   c. are aimed at bringing about social change which will affect many people.
   d. never receive much popular support.

3 Social movements usually begin as a result of
   a. legislation in Congress.
   b. a political campaign.
   c. a mood of dissatisfaction on the part of some group.
   d. a national crisis.

4 Conditions which typically give rise to social movements include
   a. legal, social, and economic discrimination toward some group.
   b. an increase in the economic well being of the general population.
   c. a rise in the religious conscience of the population.
   d. sensitivity of national politicians to the issue.

5 Social forces in the post-World War II era which gave impetus to the women's movement included
   a. working wives and mothers returning to full time housework.
   b. the increase in the number of men attending college.
   c. the new generation of young women who became involved in other social movements.
   d. the changing image of women as depicted on television.

6 The role of women has changed as a result of the women's movement in that
   a. women now enter all occupations and professions as readily as men.
   b. authority in the family is more evenly shared by husband and wife.
   c. women now do much less of the work around the house and with the kids.
   d. it is much more clearly understood and appreciated by men.

POSTTEST ANSWERS

1 d (obj. 1, TV)
2 c (obj. 2, TV)
3 c (obj. 3, TV)
4 a (obj. 4, TV)
5 c (obj. 5, TV)
6 b (obj. 6, TV)

26

Small Town Life

SOCIOLOGICAL PERSPECTIVE

Most Americans live in cities or suburbs. Most national concerns—energy, crime, sports, education, minorities, finance, and more—arise in and are dealt with in the urban arena. What about the small proportion of Americans still living in small towns? How do they live? What is the impact of urban America upon their lives?

This lesson will focus upon a small town in Texas and upon the nature of life in that town. It is not necessarily the average small American town. But it is not part of a metropolitan area. It is too far from a large city for people to make frequent trips to shop, visit physicians, or attend the movies. Local business and industry are not dependent upon nearby urban centers, tourism, or the military.

This lesson will raise the question, "Is life really different in small towns than it is in cities?" A second question to be asked is, "Is life in small towns as good as most people think it is?" Or is there a mythology of small town life quality? We will also examine the sense of community which prevails in a small town and contrast that with how people interact in the cities.

LEARNING OBJECTIVES

Knowledge Objectives

1 Define small town in terms of size and location.

2 Identify several advantages of small town life.

3 Identify several disadvantages of small town life.

4 Identify the dominant process in population growth in the past half century.

5 Identify several effects of urbanism upon small towns.

6 Contrast the nature of interpersonal relationships in small towns and cities.

7 Explain how the myth of small town uniqueness continues.

8 Explain the continuing role of the institution of religion in small town life.

Attitudinal Objectives

1 Develop a greater awareness of the commonality of most Americans, whether small town or urban, in dealing with human problems and social realities.

2 Develop a better awareness and appreciation of the sources of provincialism in small town populations.

KEY TERMS

Small town   A population of 500 to 25,000, not within the orbit of a large city, a place smaller than a small city.

Urbanism   The movement of population to urban centers.

Quality of life   The level of living, including housing, food, medical care, educational services, air, water, privacy, recreational services.

READING ASSIGNMENT

Additional Reading, "In Search of Small Town America"

READING FOCUS QUESTIONS

1 Contrast urban and small town life in terms of privacy, social pressure, and access to amenities.

2 What are some urban developments which affect small town life?

3 Describe some differences in the nature of interpersonal relationships in small towns and large cities.

TV FOCUS QUESTIONS

1 Why is the definition of "small town" difficult?

2 What do people in small towns say that their lives focus upon?

3 How have such factors as national TV programs affected small town life?

4 What are the most obvious differences in small town life?

5 What are some advantages and disadvantages of small town life?

6 What is the role of religion in small town life?

7 What is the status of minority groups in small towns?

OPTIONAL ACTIVITIES

1   Ask three people who grew up in a small town and three people who grew up in a city about their experiences. Compare them in terms of advantages in education, recreation, entertainment, and other variables they may mention.

2   Ask five people who live in the city if they would like to move to a small town. Ask them why.

POSTTEST

Multiple Choice

1   A small town is a
    a. population under 10,000 near a large city.
    b. population under 25,000 not near a large city.
    c. suburb under 25,000.
    d. population 25,000 to 50,000.

2   Advantages of small town life include
    a. less traffic and shorter distance to work.
    b. better shopping and health care.
    c. more privacy and freedom of choice.
    d. better race relations and economic opportunities.

3   Disadvantages of small town life include
    a. limited choices and personal freedom.
    b. loss of identity.
    c. reduction of open space and green areas.
    d. loss of contact with national issues.

4   The major movement of population movement in the past half century has been
    a. urban to rural.
    b. urban to suburban.
    c. urban to urban.
    d. rural to urban.

5   The major effect of the process of urbanism upon small towns has been
    a. the growth of suburbs.
    b. crowding due to population growth.
    c. the growth of technology in industry, communication, and entertainment.
    d. air and water pollution.

6 Small town and urban interpersonal relationships differ in that
   a. one is personal and face-to-face and the other is formal and segmented.
   b. the kinds of concerns people have are different.
   c. social class is less significant in small towns.
   d. people have a greater sense of belonging in urban areas.

7 The prevailing myth of small town uniqueness and difference from urban life is based upon
   a. the continuing isolation of small town people from national issues and problems.
   b. the experience which most urban people have had in small towns.
   c. the 19th century imagery of isolated, spatially distinct towns.
   d. the lack of influence of mass communication and bureaucracy upon small town life.

8 The role of churches in small town life includes
   a. unifying the total community.
   b. providing focal points for interaction within various groups.
   c. including everyone in community life.
   d. breaking down racial and economic barriers.

POSTTEST ANSWERS

1 b (obj. 1, TV)
2 a (obj. 2, TV, Additional Reading)
3 a (obj. 3, TV, Additional Reading)
4 d (obj. 4, TV, Additional Reading)
5 c (obj. 5, TV, Additional Reading)
6 a (obj. 6, TV)
7 c (obj. 7, TV)
8 b (obj. 8, TV)

In Search of Small Town America

Urbanization has been the dominant social process in the United States in the past 40 years. Population has moved to urban areas. Education, media, entertainment, sports, medicine, finance—all of these are dominated by forces in urban centers. America is, in effect, an urban nation. It is city freeways, factories, high-rise apartments and office buildings, *Sixty Minutes, The Wall Street Journal,* General Motors, the New York Yankees, the Boston Celtics, and the Houston Medical Center. All roads lead to the city, whatever the pursuit. Information, power, influence, wealth, ideas, problems—these are within the cities and move from city to city, skipping over small town America as they move.

What is the impact of urbanization upon those still living in small town America? Rather obviously, the activities of urban America in the stock market, in corporate headquarters, and at ABC central have far-reaching effects upon small town America. Energy, inflation, politics, and international relations have effects upon small town America.

Surveys indicate that although over 70% of Americans live in cities, only about 15% think of cities as the most desirable place to live. No doubt many of these are thinking of small town America. But is there something left in small town America that is still different from urban America? Is there still an American dream to be found there, a dream of tranquility, privacy, freedom from traffic, smog, crime, and noise? Do people really experience lives which are more slowly paced, more neighborly? Is it safer in the streets at night? Is the air cleaner? Are the schools better?

Small towns historically offer less privacy for individuals than urban areas offer. The massive size, density, and movement of urban populations in daily, routine activities make it possible for the individual to become lost in the crowd. The anonymity provides privacy. Varied and complex schedules— shift work, night school, organizational meetings—further the likelihood that neighbors pass as ships in the night without more than occasional conversation or greetings. The many options for work, recreation, and other involvements in the city divide a neighborhood into many parts which rarely coordinate. Where one works, how much money one makes and other variables such as marital status, church membership or preference, political beliefs, attitudes toward abortion, homosexuality, and the draft all are more likely to be unknowns in the social identity of the urban person.

It is possible for the urban person to have a closely knit group of friends with whom he shares intimacy, values, ideas and behavior and yet have the community as a whole not know of these things. Conversely, in a small town it is usually quite difficult to associate with anyone without everyone knowing about it. Cars are seen in driveways. Couples are observed in the local cafe or movie theater. Ministers, attorneys, physicians, mayors, and policemen all know about everyone in town. One's affair is everyone's affair, whether it is sexual, financial, or purely social.

Individual rights are likely to be restricted in small town life. Life style options are more limited. Social pressure to conform is greater. There are more people with a view of others' lives, not only in the backyard but at school, work, church, and on lovers' lane. The conventional wisdom as it relates to such issues as pornography, civil rights, abortion, mental illness, and cohabitation without marriage will be more narrow and more influential. One who wishes to behave somewhat differently may face the choice of being labeled different, talked about and perhaps avoided socially or limiting his different behavior to very private groups and occasions.

There is less room at the top in a small town. Those at the top are more highly visible to the total community. The young banker's wife who finishes her master's degree in special education, plays tennis at the club and wears sophisticated clothing may be labeled a snob. There will be only a few women in town of her social position. Some of them will be more discreet. In urban areas, such people make up entire communities and are more isolated from the broader community in their housing, play, and religious activities. Thus their privacy and personal freedom are enhanced.

Other areas of individual life affected negatively on the privacy variable in small town life are problems with children or other family members, travel plans and activities, business interests, and perhaps most significantly, the personal history of the individual or family. Either one has been in the community long enough that most of the community knows something about one's life, or if one stays long enough, the community will come to know more about one's life than would people in an urban community.

Although most of the small town citizens watch TV—the same programming available to urban people—and read papers and magazines, their interest in news is likely to be more provincial and narrow. The educational level may be such that a smaller proportion of the population read *Newsweek*, *The Wall Street Journal*, or *New Yorker*. Exposure to a wide range of opinions and information about social issues may be limited. Again, the conventional wisdom may be more restricted and narrow. The continuum relating to what is acceptable to community standards may be much shorter. Decisions about what is proper have been made; some long ago. Routine activities and subjects of conversations may be such that open and free discussion of controversial topics is quite limited. Issues or concerns which are common to most of the small town population may more likely dominate discussion in newspapers, small groups, family gatherings, and political events.

In small towns, access to amenities and some necessities, such as health care facilities and medical specialists, will typically be quite limited. Can one buy a good pizza in a small town? Probably not. Clothing stores, specialty food stores (except for the local specialty) will be few. Restaurants, clubs, movies, concerts, and tennis courts are in short supply. There is a mingling of classes in local restaurants. Bank presidents and variety store clerks have lunch at the local cafe. This also occurs in urban areas, but the people of various social classes will not know each other as in the small town. The country club is likely to be less fancy and more informal in the small town than in the city. A certain number of members are required to make it a going concern. Eligibility factors may be lower in small towns. Costs will be kept low and club policies will be determined by such considerations—all in order to attract sufficient membership. The distinction between members and non-members may be a bit blurred under certain circumstances. Non-members may merely walk on club tennis courts and play without invitation. Small town etiquette makes it more difficult for members to ask them to leave. The non-members are neighbors, customers, old high school acquaintances. It is more difficult to run a closed shop in a small town. Formalities and distinctions are reduced to local custom. The tag of snobbery can be more costly in small towns, socially and economically.

As urbanization grew in the cities and left the small towns behind and as urban problems and influences skipped across country from New York to Chicago to Los Angeles, much of the fallout landed on small town America. Inflation, high energy costs, violence on television, *Sixty Minutes* and *Dallas*, marijuana and blue denim—all of these and other elements have had effects in small town America. The mechanization of farming, the move of industry to small towns, and the use of computers in local banks all have brought urban technology to small town America.

Thus the values and concerns of small town America have changed with those of urban America. But the daily routine of the small town remains different from urban America. It is not as far to work or church, to buy groceries and gas, see movies, doctors, friends or anything else. There is of necessity a greater sense of community. The boat is smaller and therefore easier to rock. Any given issue which arises probably affects a greater proportion of the population than would the same issue in an urban area. The small town has certain over-riding and limiting concerns. It is farming and rainfall, or fishing and high tide, or ladies garments and the price of cotton. It is the new school stadium, or resurfacing the town's streets. Everyone knows the two people running for mayor or city marshal.

Concerning more formally stated sociological issues, the social organization of the small town will probably be more visible. The patterns of relationships, of power, influence and prestige are in a scene closer to the population than in an urban area. The particular prevailing patterns have been there longer and change more slowly. The age of the population is likely to be higher than in urban areas. Most of the young people have gone to the city for education and jobs. Few of them return. Those who return are likely to be further isolated from the locals. Education, experience in the city, awareness of options in life style, values, behavior, food, music, politics—these broaden the outlook of those who have been out in the big world and have returned to small town America.

The noise level is down, it is not far to work, you know your neighbors better, the kids are in a smaller school, and people are rarely mugged. But the trade-off is costly. Privacy is low. Everybody knows your business. A little slip can ruin a reputation. Pressures to conform are high and choices are limited. It is three hours to a heart specialist or to get braces for the kids. There is no airline service and Sears does not deliver to your front door. Your first husband and his relatives live around the corner. There is no public or private facility for mental health care. The only lawyer in town is also in real estate or has a drinking problem. Choices are limited. It is a long way to a pro ball game of any kind.

Many of those 70% of Americans who live in urban America—some of whom lived as children in small town America and think they would like to get back there—may find a long term visit to small town America disappointing. It seems on the whole that all of America is an urban village. The small towns are merely a bit farther from the center but still permeated by the concerns of the urban world. They are a bit sheltered by distance and tradition, but very much in the same boat. As much as the hurried, frustrated, over-scheduled, and noise-deadened urban American would like, upon closer examination, he probably finds that he cannot return to the haven of the small town. It is not really that safe or different. And there is not enough room there for all of us.

27

Life in the City

SOCIOLOGICAL PERSPECTIVE

There was a time when cities were viewed as centers of commerce, art, culture, growth in technology, places of excitement, pleasure, and glamour. For at least two decades, they have been seen as centers of crime, noise, pollution, and traffic. The increasing prominence of suburbs in the late 1940's signalled the beginning of the end of the city as America's dream home place. For the last few decades, a number of problems and concerns have driven population from the cities: pollution, crime, crowding, racial concerns, jobs, a yearning for green belts and open spaces.

Are the cities dead? Is life in the city as bad as the popular imagery of the city suggests? Are those left in the city after the great migration to the suburbs really trapped in ghettos? What are urban communities like? Do people still frequent city parks, walk to movies, shop in neighborhood specialty stores? How do city people feel about the city? About each other? Are they trapped? Would they leave if they could? Where would they want to go?

The focus of this lesson will be the nature and quality of life of the urban dweller. There will be special emphasis upon the social psychology of city life, that is, upon the content and effect of group-held attitudes and values upon the individual. What's out there in the city air? Is it fear, despair, loneliness? Or does the city dweller, much like his suburban or small town counterpart, think primarily about getting up and going to work tomorrow and having a cool one at the end of a summer day?

We should expect to find most city people living a bit closer to the edge of change than are rural and suburban people—and hurting a bit more from it. They will be remembering better days in the neighborhoods and in the city at large, withdrawing a bit into their private worlds while the urban storms rage about them in the racial, economic, and political worlds. Many will have a sense of being trapped, of futility, and a lowered quality of life—with little hope for improvement.

Another perspective of city life presents a different view. Some cities are revitalizing their downtown areas with new civic centers, libraries, harbors, shopping malls, and green spaces. They are building symphony halls and sponsoring human and community-centered activities which call people back to the city. While the movement is small and affects only a small proportion of the population, it may signal the beginning of a new era for the city.

A major concern is that most of the new activity downtown will be attractive to, or affordable by, only the upper portion of the class structure. The working class will stick to the suburban malls and the poor will remain locked in their present positions, untouched by it all.

This lesson focuses upon the city of St. Louis. It was chosen because it is an old, classic American city with all of the features which make cities great and most of the problems which plague cities today. This is a study of how different people feel about their lives in the city—and of the city itself.

LEARNING OBJECTIVES

Knowledge Objectives

1 Define urbanization.

2 Distinguish between *gemeinschaft* and *gesellschaft*.

3 Describe the Chicago School.

4 Describe the major changes experienced by St. Louis and other major cities in the past few decades.

5 Identify the major causes of change in the city in recent decades.

6 Describe varying effects of city life upon personal relationships and community networks.

7 Describe contrasting opinions as to the value of urban renewal to city people.

Attitudinal Objectives

1 Develop a greater awareness and appreciation of the quality of life of city people.

2 Develop a greater awareness and appreciation of the historic role of cities in America's cultural and social development and of the problems which they now face.

KEY TERMS

Urbanization   The process by which an area's population becomes larger, more dense, and more heterogeneous.

Gemeinschaft   Conditions in a small community which include a sense of belonging, loyalty, intimacy, and adherence to tradition.

Gesellschaft   Conditions in a community, usually large, which include emphasis on individualism, impersonal relationships, and a relative high rate of change which lowers commitment to traditions.

READING ASSIGNMENT

Robertson: *Sociology*, pp. 576–583

READING FOCUS QUESTIONS

1 What is urbanization?

2 What are some of the most outstanding features of urbanization in the United States in the past few decades?

3 What is the distinction between *gemeinschaft* and *gesellschaft*?

4 What is the Chicago School?

5 What are the advantages and disadvantages of living in a city?

TV FOCUS QUESTIONS

1 How has the popular view of the city changed in the last few decades?

2 What are the major problems facing St. Louis today?

3 What are some of the causes of these problems?

4 What are some effects of social class position upon how a person views life in the city?

5 What is the effect of increasing urbanization upon human relationships in the city?

6 What is the value of urban renewal projects to city dwellers?

OPTIONAL ACTIVITIES

1 Consult 1950 and 1980 census data for the city in which you live and for its suburban areas. Notice the growth or decline of each and their relationship to each other in 1950 as well as in 1980. What are the major problems of the city? How do the suburbs relate to those problems?

2 Ask ten people who live in the city what they like and dislike about living there. Ask them how it has changed in the last ten years.

POSTTEST

Multiple Choice

1 Urbanization is
   a. growth in the size of cities.
   b. an increase in size, density, and heterogeneity of cities.
   c. the increase of urban problems.
   d. the loss of green space and community ties.

2 *Gemeinschaft* describes a community in which
   a. relationships are characterized by a sense of belonging intimacy and tradition.
   b. loyalty to traditions is very low.
   c. there is a high rate of social change.
   d. there is a strong emphasis upon individualism.

3 The Chicago School's position on urbanism as a way of life
   a. concentrated upon the technological features of urban life.
   b. has never been seriously questioned by later sociologists.
   c. presented an optimistic view of urban life.
   d. was best stated by Wirth, drawing upon Tonnies and Simmel.

4 Major changes experienced by St. Louis in the past two decades include
   a. movement of the population into the city.
   b. a growth of population in both city and its suburbs.
   c. a loss of city population and growth of suburban population.
   d. a loss of total metro population to the sunbelt.

5 A major cause of population shifts and other changes in St. Louis in recent decades is
   a. the movement of industry and jobs to the suburbs.
   b. the increase of the working class in the city.
   c. the flight of the poor from expensive city housing.
   d. urban renewal projects.

6 A major effect of city life upon personal relationships is
   a. the absence of any network of support groups and institutions.
   b. the greater selectivity possible in the large population.
   c. the tendency of all city people to be hurried, anonymous and unfriendly.
   d. the higher degree of isolation than most rural people feel.

7 In regard to urban renewal, social scientists
   a. agree that it benefits all of the population.
   b. agree that it has been especially helpful to the poor.
   c. believe that it benefits residents more than businessmen.
   d. disagree sharply as to whom it benefits.

8 Participation in the benefits which the city offers seems to vary largely along the continuum of

   a. religious affiliation.

   b. length of time one has lived in the city.

   c. social class membership.

   d. political affiliation.

POSTTEST ANSWERS

1 b (obj. 1, Text, p. 576)
2 a (obj. 2, Text, p. 582)
3 d (obj. 3, Text, p. 582)
4 c (obj. 4, TV)
5 a (obj. 5, TV)
6 b (obj. 6, TV)
7 d (obj. 7, TV)
8 c (obj. 7, TV)

28

Urban Problems

SOCIOLOGICAL PERSPECTIVE

World population continues to grow at an alarming rate. This causes both rural and urban problems. Most of the rural people of the world do not have access to a drink of pure water. The hearts of the world's great cities beat painfully with a continued increase of the disenfranchised. There is a complex relationship between rural and urban. One has the food and natural resources. The other has the technology, finance, and management skills. The problems of the cities belong not merely to the cities but to the entire society in which they are found.

After a brief examination of world population, this lesson looks closely at the condition of U.S. cities, the major problems which they face, and their probable future.

Cities are caught in the larger problems of our times: inflation, energy shortages, rising expectations from various conflicting groups, and a growing self-centeredness which seems to characterize many of these groups.

This lesson raises and struggles with several difficult and complex questions: How severe is the "urban crisis"? Is it inevitable within the nature of the city (as reflected in its history) that there will be much crime, pollution, crowding? Do cities develop along some scale from newborn to boomtown to incipient decline? Will Dallas be the Detroit of 2000? Finally, are the cities to be a permanent repository for the poor? This lesson presents the views of some leading social scientists on the cities' problems and their future.

LEARNING OBJECTIVES

Knowledge Objectives

1 Define demography.

2 Describe the causes of rapid population growth.

3 Explain the theory of demographic transition.

4 Describe U.S. demographic characteristics.

5 Describe the "strip cities" of the United States.

6   Identify the primary urban problem of the United States.

7   Explain the complex relationship between the poor and the cities.

8   Describe the nature of human relationships in the city.

Attitudinal Objectives

1   Become more aware of the nature of the population crisis world wide.

2   Develop a greater sensitivity to the problems of poor people in U.S. cities.

KEY TERMS

Demography   The scientific study of the size, composition, and distribution of population and its changes.

Zero Population Growth (ZPG)   The condition which prevails when a population remains at essentially the same level over a period of time.

Demographic transition theory   A concept which attempts to explain how the size of a population changes as it develops economically.

Strip City   A U.S. urban area with at least one million population, usually including several cities.

READING ASSIGNMENT

Robertson: *Sociology,* pp. 565–576, 584–589

READING FOCUS QUESTIONS

1   What is demography?

2   What is the theory of demographic transition?

3   What are the causes of rapid population growth in the world?

4   What are the demographic characteristics of today's U.S. population?

TV FOCUS QUESTIONS

1   What is a "strip city?"

2   What is the major element in America's urban crisis?

3   What are some important features in the relationship between the cities and their non-city environments?

4   What are some consequences of the flight of the affluent from the cities?

5   What kinds of severe urban problems have already been solved?

6   What has been the impact of urban renewal upon the cities?

7   What factors seem significant in determining the future of U.S. cities?

OPTIONAL ACTIVITIES

1   Ask a number of people such as policemen, firemen, news reporters and others who are on the ground level of the urban scene about the kinds of problems they see daily and the people who are involved in them.

2   Read the daily papers of five major cities for a week and keep a log of the problems of those cities as reported in the news.

POSTTEST

Multiple Choice

1   Demography is the scientific study of
   a. food problems.
   b. population.
   c. energy.
   d. ecology.

2   The main cause in rapid population growth is
   a. the increase in the ratio of births to deaths.
   b. the rise in technology.
   c. the religious and political ideologies.
   d. the value systems of individuals.

3   Stage three in the theory of demographic transition is usually found in
   a. developing nations.
   b. large, growing nations.
   c. advanced, industrial societies.
   d. small, backward societies.

4   Concerning the median age of the U.S. population,
   a. there has been little change in 25 years.
   b. it is now about 30 and at its historical high.
   c. it is at 25 and growing lower.
   d. it is lower than most other countries.

5   "Strip cities" refers to
   a. a metro area with an elongated shape on the map.
   b. urban areas such as Vegas and Miami.
   c. urban regions which stretch from one city to another.
   d. a city of at least one million.

6 The primary urban problem of the cities in the United States today is
   a. traffic.
   b. crime.
   c. pollution.
   d. poor people.

7 The major problem cities have with the poor is
   a. changes in the work world which make it difficult for cities to employ the poor.
   b. the unwillingness of the poor to work.
   c. the lack of existing housing for the poor.
   d. the physical decay in the inner city.

8 The major effect of city life upon human relationships seems to be that
   a. it causes all of them to be brief and impersonal.
   b. while creating more categories of people, it presents a wide variety of options for social interaction.
   c. most do not have a sense of community.
   d. there are severe spatial limitations on the development of friendships.

POSTTEST ANSWERS

    1 b (obj. 1, Text, p. 566)
    2 a (obj. 2, Text, p. 567)
    3 c (obj. 3, Text, p. 572)
    4 b (obj. 4, Text, p. 573)
    5 c (obj. 5, TV)
    6 d (obj. 6, TV)
    7 a (obj. 7, TV)
    8 b (obj. 8, TV)

29

Social Change

SOCIOLOGICAL PERSPECTIVE

In some societies the rate of change is very slow. The Bakhtiari of Northern Persia have experienced only one significant change in their culture in 10,000 years: the addition of pack animals. Among the desert people of the Kalahari, where daily survival remains the same struggle generation after generation, there is very little change.

The rate of change varies with such elements as technology, demography, political ideology, ecology, and religion. U.S. culture has always been characterized by change. In the past few decades this change has been very rapid.

Many changes are superficial. Stop signs are now red instead of yellow. Mail boxes are blue instead of army green. Icemakers have replaced the twelve-by-twelve card Mom placed in the window to tell the ice man how much ice to leave. There are ball point pens, plastic, television, and countless kinds of electronic whizzos. But there have been internal, behavioral changes of much greater significance. These include how neighbors relate to each other, how people feel about politicians, physicians, clergymen, and professional athletes. There have been changes in how families function, in the roles of men and women, and in attitudes toward work.

This lesson examines social change, its causes and effects. It looks at technology, population, values—and at a special effect of very rapid change called "anomie."

LEARNING OBJECTIVES

Knowledge Objectives

1 Define social change.

2 Describe the major theories of social change.

3 Identify some major sources of social change.

4 Describe the nature of social change in the United States in recent decades.

5 Describe a special effect of very rapid social change known as "anomie."

Attitudinal Objectives

1   Develop a greater awareness and appreciation of the great amount of change experienced by many Americans and of the effect that change has upon their attitudes and behavior.

2   Become more aware of the rate of social change as the source of anxieties in yourself.

KEY TERMS

Social change   The variations in the patterns of behavior, institutions, and social organizations.

Conflict perspective   A view of society which sees conflict as a permanent and natural part of the system, a valuable source of social change.

Functionalist perspective   A view of society which emphasizes the working relationships among various elements in the system and the value of equilibrium to the maintenance and progress of the system.

Anomie   A condition in society in which many individuals feel that the rules are not valid, do not work for them, and that groups and organizations may not be depended upon for social and psychological support.

READING ASSIGNMENT

Robertson: *Sociology*, pp. 507–531

READING FOCUS QUESTIONS

1   What is social change?

2   What is the distinction between conflict and functionalist theories?

3   What are the major sources of change?

4   What are some predictions about the future of technology and culture?

TV FOCUS QUESTIONS

1   What are the fundamental social changes which have taken place in the United States since World War II?

2   What accounts for the "generation gap" in U.S. culture?

3   In what sense were the World War II years a watershed in cultural development in the United States?

4   What is the relationship between technology and culture in post-World War II American society?

5 What were the effects of demographic changes in post-World War II America?

6 What is the meaning of "anomie" and how is it expressed in contemporary U.S. society?

OPTIONAL ACTIVITIES

1 Watch a movie made before 1950. Note language, customs, dress, values in family life, law enforcement, entertainment, religion, and advertising. Compare this to your familiar world today.

2 Talk with someone over 60 about the music, language, jokes, behavior patterns and community life of their early adulthood. Ask how those have changed.

POSTTEST

Multiple Choice

1 Social change is
   a. about the same in all societies.
   b. more rapid in industrialized societies.
   c. more permanent in industrialized societies.
   d. similar in agricultural and industrialized societies.

2 Understanding social change is difficult because
   a. no factors have been isolated which cause it.
   b. scientists are not as interested in causes as effects.
   c. it involves such complex and varied factors.
   d. it is to difficult to observe.

3 As perspectives on social change, the functionalist and the conflict perspectives differ in that
   a. one sees conflict as undesirable and the other as inevitable.
   b. one emphasizes the functions of social institutions and the other emphasizes equilibrium among them.
   c. one is more clearly supported in sociological data than the other.
   d. one is more realistic and practical than the other.

4 U.S. cultural change has been
   a. limited to material items.
   b. primarily in the area of ideas.
   c. largely unaffected by climate and natural resources.
   d. very rapid and comprehensive in the past half century.

5 A major change in U.S. society since World War II involved the class structure in that
   a. there was an increase in the lower class.
   b. there was an increase in the upper class.
   c. the size of the middle class became much greater.
   d. more people moved closer to the poverty line.

6 A major demographic change in and immediately following World War II was
   a. the baby boom.
   b. the growth of the rural population.
   c. the decrease of the size of the suburbs.
   d. increased stability of the family.

7 *Anomie* is
   a. the feeling that there are no rules.
   b. created by very rapid social change.
   c. limited primarily to urban areas.
   d. a symptom of high social stability.

POSTTEST ANSWERS

1 b (obj. 1, Text, p. 508)
2 c (obj. 2, Text, p. 508)
3 a (obj. 3, Text, p. 519)
4 d (obj. 4, TV)
5 c (obj. 4, TV)
6 a (obj. 4, TV)
7 b (obj. 5, TV)

30

The New Society

SOCIOLOGICAL PERSPECTIVE

Considering the rapid change which U.S. society has experienced in the past few decades, it is only natural to speculate a bit about what the next few decades may hold. Most individuals have little acquaintance with or respect for the predictive powers of sociology. Yet, few major cultural developments have occurred in the past half century which were not forecast by social theorists. George Homans wrote in 1950 that the civilization which by its own progress in technology and industrialization destroys the small groups which surround individuals, and fails to replace those small groups, will leave individuals lonely and shattered, without sufficient reference to reality. Viewing recent and current rates of suicide, alcoholism, divorce, drug abuse, and other forms of pathology and social disorganization, we may become inclined to look more closely at the intellectual and analytical tools which are part of sociology.

Robert MacIver, writing also in 1950, described individuals who had no standards, no sense of continuity, no obligation, who were responsive only to themselves and lived on the thin line of sensation between no future and no past. He warned of a loss of a sense of social cohesion. Other writers such as Michael Novak, Alvin Toffler, and Vance Packard have discussed the effects of high mobility, industrialization, and runaway technology.

The Kerner Commission of 1968 warned of separate and highly unequal relations between the "have's" and the "have-not's" of our society, suggesting that the problems of poverty, social justice, and race are too pervasive and profound to be managed in traditional ways.

In spite of the sense of being trapped which many ordinary people feel, in the face of increasing rates of social problems of every kind, and with growing levels of public concern for the future, we seem still to be lacking any clear vision of what the future may really hold or of what decisions and actions have the greatest potential for improving society.

In this lesson, a number of social scientists discuss several important social trends, make some recommendations for problem solving, and even risk a few projections into the future. Society and its problems are complex. Solutions are complex and without guarantees. But this lesson does raise a simple and serious issue: the society of the future will be a result of the choices made by individuals, difficult choices relating to values. It seems logical to state that we must examine those choices and find the will to make them, or our New Society could be a product of default.

LEARNING OBJECTIVES

Knowledge Objectives

1 Describe two major functions of sociology.

2 Describe two practical uses of sociology for individuals.

3 Identify and describe five social trends in the coming decades.

4 Describe the role of sociology in anticipating the future.

5 Identify and describe some of the value choices facing Americans in the near future.

Attitudinal Objectives

1 Become more aware of the complexity of social relationships and the place of the individual in them.

2 Become more aware of the difficult choices facing individuals and of trends which are likely to affect them.

KEY TERMS

Lucid summations   Generalizations about social realities which are based upon scientific inquiry.

Value choices   Decisions about what is important, the setting of priorities by individuals and groups.

Taken-for-granted's   The rules, values of behavior patterns which most individuals assume to be appropriate in given settings.

READING ASSIGNMENT

Additional Reading, "A Value-Laden Essay On Sociological Intelligence and Social Trends and Values"

READING FOCUS QUESTIONS

1 What is meant by "sociology as critical intelligence?"

2 What are some problems in the projection of social trends?

3 What seems likely to happen to the family and other small groups?

4 What seems likely to occur in the area of class differences?

5   What are the two major variables which may determine the future and which are subject to human control?

6   What are some difficult intellectual choices likely to be made in the near future?

TV FOCUS QUESTIONS

1   What are the major functions of sociology?

2   How can sociology help ordinary people understand their world?

3   What are several social trends likely to prevail in the near future?

4   How is the problem of scarcity of natural resources going to affect attitudes and relationships?

5   Who are the people most likely to live the good life in coming decades?

6   What is likely to happen to the poor?

7   What are some difficult value choices facing Americans?

8   What are some recommendations from social scientists for improving society?

OPTIONAL ACTIVITIES

1   Examine the last six issues of *Futurist* magazine for discussions related to issues in this lesson.

2   Browse through library periodicals and major newspapers with an eye to social issues being discussed in editorials, featured on covers, and in headlines. Compare those with issues raised in this lesson.

POSTTEST

Multiple Choice

1   A major function of sociology is
   a. to learn what is real in human relationships.
   b. to manipulate human behavior.
   c. the clarification of human values.
   d. policy making for public organizations.

2   A significant function of sociology for the individual is
   a. freeing people from the tyrannies of their own group membership.
   b. making people feel a greater sense of isolation.
   c. creating greater harmony within a group.
   d. contributing to a more satisfactory life for the individual.

3 The continuing development of urbanism is likely to
   a. lead to a more limited choice of lifestyles.
   b. create a more pluralistic society.
   c. increase to move back to the country.
   d. create more social solidarity.

4 The status of the family in the near future will probably include
   a. a decreased emphasis upon family.
   b. less economic cooperation within the family.
   c. some new forms of quasi-communal living.
   d. a return to more traditional family forms.

5 The present reality of shrinking natural resources will
   a. create severe crises in society.
   b. have little long-term effect upon social values.
   c. unlikely cause social changes.
   d. be modified by technological advances.

6 Trends seem to indicate that participation in organizations such as government, voluntary associations will be
   a. about the same as today.
   b. more grass-roots, from the bottom up in nature.
   c. less affected by concerns for human needs.
   d. much lower than today.

7 The role of sociology in anticipating the future seems best described as
   a. an intellectual perspective asking the right questions about society.
   b. a discipline using the scientific method.
   c. a prophetic vision of the future.
   d. the statistical approach to social reality.

8 The most difficult choices facing society and individuals are in the area of
   a. technology.
   b. politics.
   c. values.
   d. energy.

POSTTEST ANSWERS

1 a (obj. 1, TV)
2 a (obj. 2, TV, Additional Reading)
3 b (obj. 3, TV, Additional Reading)
4 c (obj. 3, TV, Additional Reading)
5 d (obj. 3, TV, Additional Reading)
6 b (obj. 3, TV, Additional Reading)
7 a (obj. 4, TV, Additional Reading)
8 c (obj. 5, TV, Additional Reading)

A Value-Laden Essay On Sociological Intelligence and Social Trends and Values

Change is characteristic of our culture. Much of it seems to occur without reason or thought as to its purpose or consequences. It is quite usual that change is progress for some and pain for others. As we look to the next two or three decades, most of us do so with reserved optimism or outright fear. Change is so rapid. It seems out of control. We feel trapped in times and modes which we do not understand or control sufficiently for us to feel secure. Many of us operate in our daily lives with a low-grade fever or anxiety that things about us may come apart at any time.

Peter Berger has referred to sociology as "the application of critical intelligence to society." He warns that one who seriously studies the sociological perspective will find changed awareness which includes some element of self-liberation and another element of limitation. Not only are we more free to be ourselves, but we are also more aware of the fragility of relationships.

Because it deals with human relationships of all kinds—marital, economic, religious, community, play—sociology offers an intellectual tool and some lucid summations which are not to be found elsewhere. Sociology deals with behavior, relationships, values, exchange, patterns, rules, change, conflict, and processes. Often accused of being too broad, hard to define, and "the sociology of everything," sociology may be the discipline which offers the most useful insights into the nature of our complex society. (If it had been simple, Comte wouldn't have needed both Latin and Greek to name it!)

If we draw a circle about Mills' intersection of history and biography which takes into account American society from 1930 to 1980, we have included some very major social and cultural changes which have been examined in this course. Understanding the recent past and the present occupies much of our attention. But we are also concerned about the future. What changes are we likely to see if we draw the circle a bit larger to include the next twenty or thirty years? Merely by extending present trends which are highly visible and measurable, we can anticipate some changes. In addition, we may, for the fun or fear of it, speculate a bit in a not too irrational manner about where we may be going. An important reservation to be noted here and examined in more detail shortly is that nothing in the social order is inevitable. The projection of trends is based upon a reasoned analysis of the past and present. Projections are highly vulnerable to error. One important source of this vulnerability is the impact of the projections themselves upon the social scene and the collective consciousness.

Anticipating what may be often changes what will be. Now we turn to a not too casual and, hopefully, provocative description of what may or will be in the new society ahead of us.

Most relationships in the world of work, medicine, entertainment, recreation, and religion will increase in fragmentation. They will be secondary, surface, instrumental, and unsatisfying to the human need for intimacy and belonging. The continued erosion of traditional primary relationships eventually will bring about a resurgency of the family and of small group activities in most areas of life: church, work, community. The historic, universal need for love and belonging will cause the family to survive, probably even thrive, as individuals build secure refuges from an urban world of complexity and formality. Yet, each individual, each family, will be under more freedom and greater necessity to form personal standards of values and behavior.

The new society will be more pluralistic than the United States of the 1960's and 1970's. Alternative life styles will continue and increase. Work schedules and traditions will continue to become more flexible and varied; four day work weeks, shared jobs, parents with days off in the middle of the week for child care activities, year round use of school facilities, and other changes designed to meet individual and family needs and to conserve energy.

Limited natural resources will curtail the high living and pleasure orientation, at least in terms of consumption of goods. We should become a less hedonistic culture. New traditions should emerge to replace those which faded in the 1970's.

With the scarcity of resources and ecological concerns, competitiveness for these will increase. Tensions will grow between smokers and non-smokers, truckers and 4-wheelers, job-holders and job-seekers. An older population (median age is now about 30 and soon to be 35) will grow more conservative fiscally but be more liberal morally and ethically.

For those individuals with jobs (the good jobs will be for the well trained in science, technology, and management) the culture will offer excitement, diversity, challenge, and fulfillment. Work will be easier, technological conveniences now barely conceived will be a reality. But they will have to face some hard intellectual, moral choices. Limitations imposed by population and natural resources will necessitate the creation of higher barriers between the "have's" and the "have-not's," unless our society, in its hard look at the future, makes choices that really conserve energy, money, and human potential. Given the historical track record of Americans (and this can, of course, change), it seems unlikely that we will decide to share the wealth—even among ourselves. We are far more likely to see today's power and wealth (as well as today's poverty) maintained in its present form. Some very fundamental things have happened to U.S. culture since 1940 and all of those combined have not changed the relative position of the "have's" and the "have-not's." Individual life chances are highly predictable based upon current social class status.

More and more we will see a society based upon the survival of the fittest concept—in terms of economic and social resources. There will be a permanent underclass based both upon economic realities and social deficiencies of individuals. The American ethic which has always spoken of equal opportunity and helping the fellow in need will decline. We will become accustomed to an underclass, hardened to the needs of the poor, even more interested in self-survival than now. The problems of loneliness, isolation and anomie will increase. The pathologies of drug abuse, alcoholism, suicide, and divorce will increase.

There will be a redefinition of pleasure in that somewhere in the extension of pleasure seeking as a primary goal in life, the relativity and elusiveness of that goal will become painfully obvious and the national consciousness will return to rationality and the intellect. Hopefully, this return will occur somewhere short of the discovery of the "absolute happiness pill" or the return of the Roman gladiators.

People will become more and more critical of their time-use in voluntary activities. Traditional participation in formal church services will decline. The loss of tradition as motivation for participation during the sixties and seventies will pressure churches and other voluntary organizations to "get their act together" and attract people because real needs are being met; no other motivation will exist.

The implications of these trends for the importance of the sociological perspective are overwhelming. If a greater proportion of the population is becoming involved in decision making on environment, economy, ethics, work, and government, it is vitally important that they have some intellectual tools with which to work, some grasp of the larger scene. The melting pot idea has always been a myth. We are strong through our diversity—but we are also strained by it. Human relationships, value judgments, social change, structural change and its impact upon individual and daily lives are best understood and guided by the Sociological Imagination. It takes into account the underlying social realities and the complexity of human interaction and behavior. The tools of the sociologist must be involved in any reasoned, intellectual inquiry as to the nature and direction of social change.

Despite the availability of such intellectual tools and projections of problematic trends, we seem to be no nearer to solutions. Driven by greed, pleasure, and necessity, society plunges blindly on in a downhill, downstream mode which makes little use of its intellectual and rational faculties in value choices and behavioral patterns. The Kerner Commission warned in 1968 of a separate and highly unequal existence of the "have's" and the "have-not's." The problems of poverty, social justice and ignorance are too pervasive and profound—as are other problems such as pollution, energy shortages, and crime—to be managed without an all-out effort of government and the population.

Quite aside from the global problems facing the United States in the decade ahead, there are new and urgent matters which demand attention. AIDS is a disease which has no peer in the American experience. It will kill a quarter-million Americans in the next few years. A chemical or medical solution is not in sight until the mid-1990's at earliest, barring some totally unexpected breakthrough. The cost of merely treating present AIDS victims has become astronomical. The cost of research, education, and care for future victims will strain the resources and pluralistic consensus of American life.

Welfare is now clearly acknowledged to be a dismal failure. Politicians call for reforms, but the system on a national basis and in the culture of the ghetto is so entrenched that effective reform seems unlikely. Fifth-generation welfare children symbolize graphically the morass into which we have fallen.

Somewhere between the ACLU and fascism, there must be found operable solutions, a balance between individual rights and society's survival—however razor-thin. It seems obvious and a bit judgmental, but what is needed is some politicians with new thinking and courage to put these solutions above party and reelection. Of course, it will be helpful if the American public has the good sense to support them.

Society need not be left to the mercies of fate or dumb luck. There are no inherent forces or trends which are inviolate to criticism, change, adjustment. It is not inevitable that 50,000 people die on U.S. highways annually, or that veneral disease epidemics sweep the adolescent culture of America. Issues such as abortion, alcoholism, child abuse, criminal recidivism, and energy conservation can be attacked intellectually and more successfully than in the past. There are answers which are better than the conventional wisdom heretofore offered. Social theorists with a comprehensive view of social organization and the dynamics of a society, with social facts relating to various aspects of human and group behavior, are capable of predicting what may work and what has little chance of working in trying to solve our societal ills and cope with a growing complexity of human life.

Successfully meeting the challenge of the present and of the future seems to involve two major variables: values and nerve. Aleksandr Solzhenitsyn said to the Harvard graduating class of 1978: "One almost never sees voluntary self-restraint. Everybody operates at the extreme limit of those legal frames. . . . Destructive and irresponsible freedom has been granted boundless space. Society appears to have little defense against the abyss of human decadence, such as, for example, misuse of liberty for moral violence against young people, motion pictures full of pornography, crime and horror . . . Life organized legalistically has thus shown its inability to defend itself against the corrosion of evil. . . . No weapons, no matter how powerful, can help the West until it overcomes its loss of will power . . . To defend oneself, one must also be ready to die; there is little such readiness in a society raised in the cult of material well-being."

J. Bronowski wrote in *The Ascent of Man*: "I am infinitely saddened to find myself suddenly surrounded in the West by a sense of terrible loss of nerve, a retreat from knowledge into. . . . falsely profound questions about, 'Are we not really just animals at bottom?' . . . They do not lie along the line of what we are now able to know if we devote ourselves to it: an understanding of man himself. We are nature's unique experiment to make the rational intelligence prove itself sounder than the reflex. Knowledge is our destiny. Self-knowledge, at last bringing together the experience of the arts and the explanations of science, waits ahead of us."

Lest skeptics should dismiss Solzhenitsyn and Bronowski as foreign nuts who don't really know America, it should be observed that external objectivity is no doubt what is required here, that most students of behavioral and social science have for some time recognized the inherent threats to social order and the total social fabric of a cultural value system based upon self-centeredness and pleasure. The "me" generation of the 1960's and 1970's has done more to our culture than merely get us into blue jeans and disco music. It has led us to a rejection of the intellect, not only in religion and music, but in love, family, work, and other aspects of human behavior and relationships. The "now" generation, the instant happiness trip, the "help me make it through the night" ideology—these are no doubt real responses to some pain, loneliness, and despair. But they are shallow, short term, and insidious in nature.

Social systems, cultural values, political and economic ideologies—none of these is inviolate. Any of these can be changed. We are all at all times involved in creating the social realities with which we and our children will live. Social reality is produced by people. Social systems are created over time by human action. Bronowski commented in his *The Ascent of Man* that what people witness are not events but the actions of people.

Bronowski says that the ascent of man will go on but he warns that one should not assume that it will go on carried by Western civilization as we know it. The next step will be taken, but perhaps not by us. "We have not been given any guarantee that Assyria and Egypt and Rome were not given. We are waiting to be somebody's past too, and not necessarily that of our future." Bronowski further states that man is not locked into his environment, but that "his imagination, his reason, his emotional subtlety and toughness, make it possible for him not to accept the environment but to change it."

The challenge of the present and of the future must stir our sociological imaginations. Man is not locked into the trap he feels. He can, through the development of intellectual sensitivities and tools, become able to deal more effectively with the events and processes which occur in his own life and in the broader social structure.

Max Weber saw that bureaucracy and large scale organizations were the basic elements of modern political, social, and economic life. He saw one sanctuary of personal action, one area where an individual could affirm himself in a world dominated by bureaucracy: the area of choice of fundamental values. This is the last preserve of passion. Each individual bears the awful responsibility for choice and action at this ultimate level.

The world of work, education, medicine, and religion is indeed dominated by bureaucratic and formalized processes. The leisure time, individualized life style content of our culture is now dominated by the sensate mode: emotions, feelings, pleasures, fears. This dichotomy has an internal dynamics which continues to work against itself. Everyman submits to eight hours of bureaucratic work, then turns into a Jekyll-Hyde, a pleasure seeker with his mind turned off.

The more deadening the work day, the more frantic the pursuit of relief. The forms of relief found frequently have severe repercussions upon the work day: alcoholism, absenteeism, low productivity, hostility. The pleasure pursuit also affects other aspects vital to Everyman's life such as relationships in marriage and family, with friends, community and other social institutions. No society in history has managed to develp a system which gave everything to everybody. But our system advertises to everybody the good life for everybody, raising expectations to unparalleled heights. The pursuit of these cultural goodies leaves children unattended, wives (and husbands) home alone (or doing whatever), communities disorganized and social institutions in disarray.

Some *very tough intellectual choices must be made by Americans*—choices in values. Belonging and freedom are not mutually exclusive, except in their extremes. People need to belong. American culture has encouraged freedom in the extreme for almost a generation. Belonging has been hurting and with it people have been hurting. Clean air and consumption, ethical stances and pleasure are also not mutually exclusive, except, again, in their extreme forms. Decisions must be made. They have been made and are being made but it seems largely by default, drift and "getting through the night." Everyman must get above this thing and view it objectively, coldly, dispassionately, with an eye to the next bend in the road.

We need not be afraid. We are not yet trapped beyond despair. We think, therefore, we are. The history developing about us is our history. We are making it. We can make it what we choose. But somehow there must arise a consciousness of community and a sense of responsibility to that community which generates the will to make rational choices and to develop rational behavior.

We need better information—some Herman Kahn "status of the world" type of stuff—and a sociological imagination to ask the right questions about our society. Finding the answers, we need the nerve to make the choices of values that will move us toward a new society—one in which all individuals live with dignity, freedom, productivity, and responsibility for themselves and others.